TWIST OF FATE

The Moirae in Everyday Psychology

Brad Hastings

University Press of America,® Inc.
Lanham · Boulder · New York · Toronto · Plymouth, UK

Copyright © 2008 by
University Press of America®, Inc.
4501 Forbes Boulevard
Suite 200
Lanham, Maryland 20706
UPA Acquisitions Department (301) 459-3366

Estover Road
Plymouth PL6 7PY
United Kingdom

Library of Congress Control Number: 2007937976
ISBN-13: 978-0-7618-3934-7 (paperback : alk. paper)
ISBN-10: 0-7618-3934-8 (paperback : alk. paper)

⊖™ The paper used in this publication meets the minimum
requirements of American National Standard for Information
Sciences—Permanence of Paper for Printed Library Materials,
ANSI Z39.48—1984

To Maria, Adam, and Andrew

who have taught me more than they will ever know

"There is in every man a certain feeling that he has been what he is from all eternity, and by no means became such in time."
–F. W. J. Schelling (as quoted in Emerson, 1860/1981, p. 352)

"When . . . we talk of 'psychology as a natural science,' we must not assume that means a sort of psychology that stands at last on solid ground. It means just the reverse; it means a psychology particularly fragile, and into which the waters of metaphysical criticism leak at every joint, a psychology whose elementary assumptions and data must be reconsidered in wider connections and translated into other terms."
–William James (1892/1984, pp. 400–401)

Table of Contents

Acknowledgments

There are a large number of students and colleagues with whom I have discussed the ideas in this book and I am indebted to them for their keen insights and helpful comments. However, I want to single out those individuals who were critical to the completion of this project and the development of the ideas herein.

First and foremost, is Barbara Shaffer, who as a friend, colleague, and former student spent endless hours discussing ideas with me and helping me to fully develop the theory of the Moirae and its applications. She also spent her precious time reviewing rough drafts and indicating areas that needed more development and clarification. I am deeply indebted to her for her intellect, time, and friendship.

I am also grateful to Steven Quackenbush. Our enlightening discussions and intellectual jousting in graduate school, and since, laid the groundwork for many of the ideas that I have since developed. I also want to thank him for his penetrating and critical intellect, which has continuously pushed me to question my own assumptions.

Char Wedge and the students in the Honors program at Mount Aloysius College have graciously provided me with the opportunity to subject them to early drafts of this manuscript. I thank them for their patience, critiques, and lively discussions.

Susan Davis was invaluable as my editor. She helped me to produce a book that more clearly elucidates my ideas in a well-written style. I thank her for her time and advice.

Finally, I am indebted to Mount Aloysius College for providing me with the sabbatical time necessary to complete this work. I am positive that the project would have never been completed without this invaluable time to write and reflect.

Part One: The Moirae

Chapter One

Twist of Fate: An Introduction to a Classical Idea

". . . but I drifted into psychology and philosophy from a sort of fatality." – William James (1935/1996, p. 228)

A Brief Intellectual History of Fatalism

How often do we hear phrases such as "God's will," "whatever will be, will be," "it is in the stars," "follow one's destiny," "everything happens for a purpose," and "only time will tell"? Popular movies, such as the Star Wars or The Matrix series, place great emphasis on the role of fate. The astrology and tarot card industries are thriving businesses. In other words, contemporary euphemisms and popular culture signify a strong belief in fate. Belief in destiny is a central element in the *lebenswelt*, or life-world, of many individuals. More importantly, dialogue in the social sciences today is rooted in an implicit acceptance of fatalism. Despite its pervasiveness in contemporary societies, the word fate is seldom mentioned in intellectual conversation in the United States; if one appeals to fate as an explanation it is often met with polite disregard. An appeal to fatalism may indeed reflect an intellectual shallowness and the absence of critical thinking. Most educated individuals would choose to admit ignorance rather than use fate to explain broad, unresolved questions. The mere mention of destiny and "the fates" brings to mind images of TV fortune tellers, oracles, horoscopes, superstition, and astrology. In conversation with professional colleagues it is safer to disclose an affinity for professional wrestling than to argue rationally for a pro-fatalism position.

Another reason we in the social sciences generally avoid discussions of fate concerns its serious and ominous aspect, one that involves the potential abandonment of freedom and responsibility. To ascribe one's life to fate can allow apathy to predominate in the face of evil, in for example, the status quo during the civil rights struggle in America and the ideology of a political party in Nazi Germany, or as exists today, indifference to violence in Rwanda, or the Sudan. This somber and important aspect of fatalism will be addressed in later chapters. The reader is urged to remain aware of this darker side throughout the text, for as Emerson (1860/1981) so aptly stated, "They who talk much of destiny, their birth-star, etc., are in a lower dangerous plane, and invite the evils they fear" (p. 358).

However, we must also take care not to throw out the proverbial baby with the bath water. The philosophy of fatalism has an ancient and respected past, of which the existing records pertaining to it permeate our scientific, spiritual, and mythological worlds. For example, the oracle at Delphi is well-known to those familiar with Greek culture but it is also a prominent figure in Greek religion, myth, and literature. The oracle was a woman who acted as a possessed medium through whom Apollo, the god of prophecy, spoke. Travelers, military planners, and average citizens sought her advice. The Gods were personifications of fate for the Greeks. This belief is most evident in "The Moirae" or more simply, "The Fates": Clotho (the spinner), Lachesis (the drawing of lots), and Atropos (inevitability), three goddesses of the ancient Greek world, were daughters of the Nyx (night). They are most commonly envisaged as three elderly women who decide the fate of Greek citizens starting at the moment of birth; they unravel each person's destiny, including the time of death. The Moirae are so powerful that even the gods were subject to fate, whereupon even the mightiest king of the gods, Zeus, was a tool of destiny. In general, this conceptualization of fate is of a broad, impersonal force that dictates our place in the world. As Hatab (1990) has noted, the Greek notion of fate is radically different from later religious conceptualizations in which the prosaic details of our lives are God's will. Instead, the Greek sense of fate is a force that imposes various parameters upon the course of our lives. It could thus be insightful for social scientists to borrow this powerful image, with its original intention, from the cradle of Western civilization, in order to examine the boundaries of contemporary existence.

Destiny has also often been a central theme in legendary Greek tragedy. Perhaps most infamous is the lot drawn by Oedipus. The playwright Sophocles describes how Laius, King of Thebes, was warned that any son his wife bore him would one day be his murderer. A shepherd was therefore instructed to abandon the queen's first born on a mountainside. Disobeying the orders, the child was instead given to a peasant who delivered him to the King of Corinth where he was named Oedipus. As a young prince it was prophesied to Oedipus, by the Oracle at Delphi, that he would one day kill his father and marry his mother. Appalled and deeply disturbed, he purposefully left Corinth and his supposed parents intending to avoid this fate. Oedipus had an altercation with a stranger enroute to Thebes, whom he subsequently killed. The Oracle at Delphi's prophecy was now partially fulfilled, for the stranger was his true father

Laius. Oedipus later solved the riddle of the Sphinx and his reward was the kingdom of Thebes. He assumed the vacant throne and married Laius' widow Jocasta. When Oedipus eventually realized that he had fulfilled his destiny, despite having taken every precaution to avoid doing so, he blinded himself and wandered the land as a vagrant.

Homer's Iliad and Odyssey are moreover filled with allusions to fate. In the Iliad Achilles is destined to a heroic life and death. His mother knew that he was fated to die in Troy, so to protect him as an infant she dipped him into the river of Hades. But she had to hold him by his heels, and in so doing neglected his one area of vulnerability. When Achilles reached adulthood Odysseus sought him out to aid in the search for Helen of Troy. His mother disguised Achilles within a group of maidens, but cleverly, Odysseus found him and convinced him to join the search for Helen of Troy. In the Odyssey Odysseus's adventures are guided by divine forces. Throughout Homer's epic poetry humans are represented as vehicles of the divine manifestation of fate. However, Homer's poetry and the Greek myths are also guided by a sense of rationality. As Hamilton (1942) has documented, the Greek myths are not rife with magic, demonic wizards, or other instances of the "terrifyingly irrational." Greek gods are also depicted as utterly human; they serve as a mirror of men and women, and are subject to the whims of fate.

Fatalism is not unique to the Greek world. Eastern and Western religious traditions echo the wisdom and warnings of prophets, soothsayers, and omniscient gods. The first book of the Bible reads more like a preordained vision than a historical treatise. From Genesis to the Book of Job to the New Testament scriptures, there are provocative tales about destiny and how one copes with fate. Many Biblical stories can be read as the unconscious manifestation of divine purpose through the course of human events. The story of Joseph wonderfully illustrates this concept. Joseph's brothers sell him into slavery early in his life. As the years pass, ironically, he becomes a powerful administrator in the Egyptian government: the brothers who had forsaken him are eventually saved by this influential government aide. Most importantly, the characters in this story are never consciously aware of their roles in the unfolding of God's divine purpose. Even the gospels relating the story of Jesus' life are filled with allusions to destiny. One forgotten lesson about the life, and more importantly the death, of Jesus, is the necessity to accept one's ultimate fate. As Jesus hung upon the cross, he realized that to do otherwise would be irresponsible, selfish and ultimately, a rejection of God.

Eastern tradition also provides numerous mythological lessons pertaining to the influence of fate. The powerful, aggressive Shiva, the embodiment of freedom and fate, is one well-known figure. Others such as Vishnu and Maya, who purportedly ascended the stages from insects to at last man and god and woman and goddess, respectively, embody the idea of a predestined path. But perhaps the most important figure from Eastern religion is the Buddha. A central tenet of Buddhist philosophy is that suffering is our fate and our only escape from suffering is to feel compassion. Finally, the *I Ching* has traditionally served as the oracle of the East. However, Westerners have also developed a fascination with

The Book of Change, whereby even scholars such as Carl Jung have been attracted to it.

Belief in the fates has also had a significant impact on our political and historical legacies. Historically, political leaders have sought guidance from oracles and prophecy, and their decisions have helped to shape our heritage. We know that Greek and Roman leaders consulted oracles. Shakespeare's portrayal of Julius Caesar is one well-known literary example of a life organized around a fatalistic timeline. Recall the admonition: "Beware the Ides of March." Napoleon Bonaparte firmly believed he was a man of destiny, a belief that is likely to have framed his decision-making process. More recently, Adolf Hitler believed the writings of Nostradamus foretold the rise of the Third Reich, and Ronald Reagan's wife Nancy regularly consulted astrological charts. As unscientific and seemingly irrational as these methods are, it is apparent that many successful individuals seriously believe in some form of fate, just as the prominent citizens visited the oracle at Delphi. It seems that, for many of our religious and political leaders, the belief in destiny is an integral component of their *lebenswelt*.

Writers and artists have also been periodically enamored with destiny. The movement that most clearly illustrates this principle is 19th century Romanticism. Romantic artists and writers expressed a strong belief in destiny, especially with regard to love. The poetry of Keats and Shelley glorifies the concept of souls who are destined to belong together. It is interesting to note that, in our romantic endeavors, most have at some point in their lives believed in destiny. Shakespeare's *Romeo and Juliet* is the greatest example in English literature. In the college courses that I teach, I find that roughly half of my students believe they have a "soul mate" they are destined to find. This belief is astounding when one considers the divorce rate and cynicism that permeates our society. The Romantics also explored fate in other contexts; Goethe's *Young Man Werther* finds himself destined for death. While Emerson (1860/1981) writes, "When each comes forth from his mother's womb, the gate of gifts closes behind him. Let him value his hands and feet, he has but one pair. So, he has but one future, and that is already predetermined in his lobes and described in that little fatty face, pig-eye, and squat form. All the privilege and all the legislation of the world cannot meddle or help to make a poet or a prince of him" (p. 351). Keep in mind that this quote is from one of the most esteemed American essayists. Undoubtedly, 19th century intellectuals were receptive to fate as an explanation for the human condition.

Throughout history, people have appealed to fate as a powerful tool for explaining human experience in the world. Today, however, the concept is forbidden in intellectual discourse. I assert that the concept remains embedded in our theories, research, and scholarship. Moreover, I would argue that the positivistic paradigm that currently frames our beliefs in the social sciences does not provide us with the imagery or language to discuss these ideas. Let us next explore how, arguably, the most prominent of the social sciences, psychology, has addressed the role of fate in human lives.

Fate and Psychology

Those who are probably regarded as most averse to the philosophy of fatalism are scientists who seek a rationalistic and atomistic world view. Most of contemporary psychology seeks to explain human behavior and cognition through the scientific method. One sure way to evoke a vehement attack from an ordinarily sedate academic psychologist is to associate their life's work with the aforementioned TV fortune tellers, oracles, horoscopes, superstition, and astrology. If you are fortunate you will only be forced to listen to an abbreviated General Psychology lecture delineating the vast differences between pseudoscience and true science. Despite the substantial disparities between science and pseudoscience, the occult and science do share one concern: prediction. The choice of methodology is where the two fields part company. A fear of association with pseudoscience prevents psychologists from discussing the future, despite that the goal of their endeavors is prediction. The future is just too speculative.

On the other hand, psychologists have plenty to say about the past. They are prepared to discuss the latest school shooting, the sexual predilections of our presidents, the origins of the Holocaust, why O.J. Simpson was acquitted, the motives of terrorists, and other events after they have occurred. Also, psychologists feel quite comfortable when discussing general patterns of human behavior and percentage predictions on a group level, e.g., "Most poor children will benefit from Head Start academically, socially, and emotionally." However, rarely does any social scientist, and wisely so, attempt to predict the future behavior of *an individual*. The irony is that we feel quite comfortable accepting predetermination as an explanation for past behavior or as a means of describing group statistics. However, we immediately switch mental gears at the individual level by refusing to acknowledge fate, destiny, or any related concept. Yet, we still do not address the role of free will.

The gist of my argument, simply stated, is that psychologists utilize the scientific method but they behave like historians and sociologists. Psychology has an "oracle complex." The history of psychology is dominated by a reductive examination of the past. The reasons for the vast array of human behaviors vary from unconscious forces to stimulus-response connections to cognitive schemata. A focus on the past is a common thread throughout these seemingly disparate explanations of human behavior. As scientists, psychologists should be concerned with the future. No physicist would hesitate to predict the trajectory of an individual proton. However, no respectable psychologist feels comfortable predicting the fate of an individual. This situation is puzzling, since psychologists are attempting to find the *causes* of behavior and cognition using scientific research methods. The goal of our present psychological enterprise is prediction, preferably, precise prediction at the individual level of human experience. Ironically, if we are eventually successful we would become the Greek oracles we so fervently loathe!

The purpose of this book is to reconcile contemporary psychology with the ancient, and intellectually respectable, position of fatalism. If I accomplish this goal, the field of psychology, and in turn, humanity will benefit. We will then possess a meta-theory that encompasses all of psychological theory and research while providing a dramatic new paradigm for understanding human nature. Such an intellectual accomplishment will draw together all aspects of our humanity from our spirituality to our cognitive processes: from personality to biology, from social behavior to unconscious dreams and desires, put simply, by turning psychology "upside down." That is, by focusing on the future, teleological, and fatalistic explanations instead of past-oriented, causal explanations, all of our theories and research may fall into place. The time has come to set aside our prejudice against fatalism and follow our destiny!

If the reader agrees to follow the theoretical path I have cleared, an initial important question arises which is: where does a work like this fit into the field of psychology? The themes I address draw heavily from the language and traditions of Romanticism and Nativism. As discussed earlier, Romanticism was a 19th century intellectual movement that attempted to reconcile ideas of love, freedom, and destiny outside the boundaries of formal reason. Kirk Schneider (1998), in the flagship journal of the American Psychological Association, has urged psychologists to adopt the Romantic tradition, a tradition that views the world in a fundamentally different way from Enlightenment rationality and causal explanations. As he argues, "For the Romantic, however, the world was much too broad and interconnected to be 'dissected' in such a way" (p. 278). He declares that the Romantic view focuses on relevant characteristics that contrast with Enlightenment rationality. These include "the interrelated wholeness of experience, access to such wholeness by means of tacit processes—affect, intuition, kinesthesia, and imagination" (p. 278).

This "Romantic Psychology" as Schneider explains, includes influences from existential, humanistic, narrative, transpersonal, and other sources within psychology. Therefore, theorists as disparate as Abraham Maslow, Rollo May, William James, and Edmund Husserl are included. From phenomenology to humanistic psychology, there is an emphasis in these theories on the holistic *lebenswelt* of the person. Theorists in the Romantic tradition also encourage psychologists to rely and draw important ideas from the humanities and religious traditions instead of exclusively adopting a scientific approach to the study of human existence. Romantic psychologists are able to draw from the rich traditions found in literature, philosophy, history, and mythology. I would therefore add the names of psychoanalytic psychologists such as Sigmund Freud, Carl Jung, and Henry Murray, to the list of psychologists in the Romantic tradition. Despite their medical and scientific training, these psychologists were open to knowledge from other disciplines in order to more accurately capture and explain the human condition.

Perhaps the most important aspect within the Romantic tradition, whether it is the poetry of Lord Byron, the philosophy of Sartre, or the essays of Emerson, is its emphasis on the individual. We seem, however, to have lost the person in psychology. Our research, theories, and official positions are based on aggregate data which is never applicable to any particular person. In my ten years of teaching college classes, the most consistent quality I find in my students is that, foremost, they are interested in themselves. This is not to say that they are profoundly self-absorbed, but rather that they seek explanations for their behavior, attitudes, and beliefs, and those of their family and friends. Furthermore, this is most true for the psychology majors. However, what these students discover is a disappointing lack of insight into why they behave and think as they do. Instead, I provide them with "fictional averages" about how most people respond, most of the time, to particular situations. Such information is invaluable to the industrial/organizational psychologist or an administrator designing policies that affect people on an aggregate level. However, the value of our data vanishes as soon as we try to explain why a particular person behaves in a particular way.

The situation within psychology has deteriorated so greatly that even the subfield which has traditionally emphasized the individual person more than any other, clinical/counseling psychology has also moved dramatically away from treating people as individuals. Health care costs, HMOs, and other societal pressures have compelled therapists to increasingly move away from "depth psychology," which emphasizes a person's life story, toward medical and cognitive/behavioral therapies supported by aggregate research data. I do not suggest that these approaches are never valuable. Indeed, any solution to human suffering is welcome, despite its theoretical approach. However, even the general public is becoming aware of the limits of these interventions. Prozac, Ritalin, and desensitization are not the answers to all of our problems.

For research psychologists and social scientists to refocus on the person's *lebenswelt* would be an invaluable benefit to the understanding of human nature. I hope to contribute to such a leap forward by providing a meta-theory that encompasses the valuable advances of aggregate data research, allowing us to address the individual, and thus return the person to psychology.

The meta-theory that I advance is also indebted to the philosophical tradition of Nativism, which stresses the importance of the innate characteristics of human beings for determining cognition and behavior. This position is often placed in contrast with the empiricism adopted by Aristotle and Locke; they regarded the person as a "tabula rasa" or blank slate; from day one henceforth the environment was to create the individual through experience and learning. Behaviorists during the 20th century advanced this concept to its logical conclusion exclusively emphasizing environmental factors such as classical and operant conditioning as being the sole determinants of behavior. Indeed, these philosophers and psychologists have illustrated the importance of the environment as a determinant of behavior. However, Nativists have also made important contributions.

Socrates was a Nativist who encouraged that one must "know thyself." He proposed that knowledge is hidden within us and he sought to be a "midwife of thought." Plato, Socrates' pupil and successor, adopted Socrates' Nativism and later proposed the "allegory of the cave": Imagine a person chained in a cave; all that the person can see are the shadows of objects outside. If the person were to be freed from the chains to leave the cave, that person would see the real objects or forms, and realize that previous sensory impressions had been merely illusory. The forms are essentially the eternal reality that underlies all appearances.

During the Renaissance, Descartes attempted to strip philosophy of its metaphysical ideas and begin anew. He began to doubt the existence of everything. There was only one thing he could be sure existed; that he was thinking his thoughts. "*Cogito ergo sum.*" This concept became the foundation for his philosophy. He eventually realized that there were fundamental human ideas that could not possibly be learned through the environment and yet were fundamental to human existence; he concluded that the ideas are innate. They included God, geometry, infinity, and unity. Kant extended this idea by advancing the notion of "a priori concepts" such as cause, totality, negation, and nonexistence, which filter our view of reality. Finally, Leibniz portrayed the human mind as containing inborn predispositions called Monads. These immutable elements of the mind comprise all cognition and behavior and are active at different levels of consciousness. Leibniz's ideas are likely a precursor to Freud's conceptualization of the unconscious.

A number of contemporary psychologists have also adopted the Nativist positions. Linguist Noam Chomsky (1966) has proposed a "language acquisition device" which provides humans with the capacity to learn language. Piaget (1936) viewed each chronological period of the child as the unfolding of a new cognitive schema. More recently, evolutionary psychologists and numerous trait theorists have also adopted Nativist ideas in order to explain human vicissitude.

Despite having sympathy for the Romantic and Nativist positions, I do not want my empirically-oriented colleagues to decide to spend valuable time reading some other work. I too was trained as a research-oriented psychologist immersed at the deep end of the rationalist and empiricist pool. We will, however, discover that the concept of fate not only haunts the houses of Nativism and Romanticism but also the mansions of Empiricism and Rationalism.

Empiricism and Rationalism are rooted in the ideas of observation and logical deduction. Contemporary scientific methods utilize the tool of logical positivism in order to "discover" the natural laws of the universe and report how various phenomena operate; this same theoretical approach and its associated methodology are employed in psychology to construct a model of the human being. Perhaps the best-known example is cognitive psychology. The roots of this subfield lie in the behaviorism of John Watson and B. F. Skinner, whereby the external environment provides rewards, punishment, and various reinforcement schedules useful to *predict* future behavior. This model was most effective in explaining animal learning; however, behaviorists during the 1960s began to employ hypothetical, internal, "cognitive" constructs to tackle problems such as human language and memory. There is a long history of this tendency within behaviorism dating back to Edward Tolman (Thorne & Henley, 2005). However, not until the 1960s did operationally-defined cognitive constructs become the standard operating procedure.

The metaphysics of fatalism was present when B. F. Skinner developed an operational conditioning theory that could be utilized to explain everything from pigeon-guided missiles to utopian societies. Philosophically, behaviorism contained the ultimate aberration of freedom and a complete acceptance of fatalism. Cognitive psychology has extended this metaphor and philosophical position to the person's interior. According to the cognitive psychologist, not only does the environment dictate our fate but so does our interior landscape of schemas, scripts, and associationist networks. We therefore find that the traditions of Empiricism and Rationalism, as currently manifest in the logical positivism of contemporary psychology, are also indebted to the ancient position of fatalism.

To summarize, the position I adopt draws most obviously from the legacies of Romanticism and Nativism. However, logical positivism is also metaphysically rooted in fatalism. The difference seems to be that Romanticism and Nativism are more likely to embrace their ancient relative, while Empiricism and Rationalism shun fatalism like a kissing cousin. But by using these philosophical resources, we can develop a psychological meta-theory that allows for a more accurate conceptualization of contemporary psychology. Let us now explore the tenets of an unconscious fatalism in chapter two.

Chapter 2

Bound by Fate: How the Unconscious Determines our Lives

". . . life must be understood backwards, but . . . it must be lived forwards."
–S. Kierkegaard (1843/1959, p. 89)

We have briefly examined the intellectual history of fatalism and explored how the fatalistic position advocated here evolves from the traditions of Romanticism and Nativism. The purpose of the present chapter is to precisely delineate the tenets of this new meta-theoretical approach, which I shall call "The Moirae," (pronounced "Mor-ay"). In other words, what are the parameters for "explaining" humans from this perspective? The main tenets of the Moirae are outlined in this chapter. However, more explicit clarification is provided in later chapters. I also discuss two examples of the Moirae (i.e., death and sex) that operate on a quotidian basis for nearly all of us. As a result, these Moirae have been more fully examined by artists, writers, scientists, psychologists, and spiritual leaders.

Tenets of an Unconscious Fatalism

1. Unconscious Collective Processes

The Moirae is a label useful for organizing and describing a vast array of psychological processes that direct our lives at the unconscious level. Although these phenomena have been personified and objectified throughout the ages, as shown in chapter one, *it is most useful to conceptualize the Moirae as processes* not things, persons, or noumena. An incessant problem with labeling any abstract idea is that it then becomes objectified (or personified) by the reader. One tends to discuss and view the concept as a "thing." In our case, however, such an approach would be completely inappropriate, since the Moirae are an evanescent process. Their very nature is one of flux, change, and process. Inasmuch as we require narrative to convey this idea within these pages, the use of language to discuss the process will inevitably limit and weaken its essence. Many will want to reduce this elusive nature to the word itself. The reader is hereby forewarned that any attempt to concretely define the Moirae precisely will result in a sparring contest with your local deconstructionist.

Of course, by merely discussing the contours and illuminating the vague shapes of these processes we open ourselves to critique from psychological empiricists who require that we operationally define all concepts in order to conduct research studies to determine their validity. We must remind our empirically-oriented colleagues that we are discussing a meta-theoretical, philosophical framework. Therefore, although the language we use will tempt us to concretize these ideas, we must return vigilantly to recall their fluidity.

A central feature of the Moirae is that *they operate simultaneously on many unconscious, psychological levels*. These include the physiological, behavioral, cognitive, and spiritual levels. As a result, our attempts to articulate and communicate these processes have manifested in a plethora of ways, depending on which level of analysis we have chosen to employ. Psychologists typically focus on only one (e.g., neuroscience), or possibly two, levels of analysis (e.g., neural basis of memory). In reality, most researchers devote their time exclusively to one specific aspect of one level of analysis. The neuroscientist who studies the chemical basis for cyclical processes in the suprachiasmatic nuclei typically has little basis for a discussion with a personality psychologist (or even other neuroscientists) on factor-analyzing the core components of personality. Specialization is productive for collecting facts within a research area. However, the result is that we commonly reject or ignore the similarities that traverse all levels of the analysis. I will not belabor this point here, however, since others have duly noted the problem. Nevertheless, scholars typically select the inductive approach in order to uncover common principles and ideas across levels of analysis. I advocate here a more deductive approach. Therefore, let us adopt the philosophical concepts present in the Moirae *on faith*, as a thought experiment, and discover which preexisting empirical research is consistent with the theory. Although such a process may cause some to object because of a vaguely recollected principle implanted during an early introduction to scientific principles, my rationale for employing this technique is sound. Others will insist that they are scientists not involved in the business of faith. As philosophers of science have revealed, and most lay people understand, every enterprise is rooted in faith. Even scientists must accept certain principles on faith, such as empiricism and causality, two philosophical notions that cannot be decisively proven. What I ask the reader to accept is no more incredulous; I am essentially attempting to *radically alter the entire psychological enterprise* toward a teleological explanation of the human condition and, as a result, the old philosophical rules must bend or break. If the system I present explains the vast majority of research in a comprehensive and clear manner, we must accept it and not be blinded by our past assumptions.

We should moreover consistently move across the levels of explanation already imposed upon psychology, not seeking to locate commonalities and then devise a theory to inevitably reflect *only* the philosophical biases and assumptions implicit in the levels of analysis. Instead, we begin with the ancient and philosophically-noble idea of fatalism; we incorporate that which psychoanalysis has revealed to us about the nature of the unconscious, and then seek to elucidate the processes which pull us toward a future state. The existing psychological research is likely to emit a different hue if one has the courage to try on new philosophical spectacles.

Finally, *the Moirae originate from a universal collective* common not only to humans but also to animals, inorganic objects, the Earth, and the Universe. They are totality and reality. They are the Gods, Buddha, and Christ. As human beings we are often limited to understanding the Moirae in an anthropomorphic light. As a result, our discussions of the Moirae will focus on the psychological experience of these processes; however, the Moirae are not inherently psychological processes but are, as we have mentioned above, the nature of reality itself. This statement may at first seem contradictory to the reader. However, upon closer examination, a subtle but important distinction will become apparent. We are examining a universal force (i.e., reality) from a psychological perspective. As discussed earlier, from this orientation the Moirae are more accurately characterized as processes; their true "nature" is beyond human language and comprehension. We are aware only of our phenomenological experience of the processes of reality.

Jung (1919/1971) noted that the collective unconscious contained archetypes common to all humans. His mistake was to not ground these concepts more firmly in our material being. The Moirae are in our neurotransmitters, atoms, sky, dirt, desert, and asteroids. The Moirae are manifested not just in human experience, but also in nature itself. Therefore, we need to recognize that nature is a mirror. This is a fact that Transcendentalists Henry David Thoreau and Ralph Waldo Emerson fully realized. Thoreau (1862/1993) writes ". . . in Wildness is the preservation of the world" (p.61), while Emerson asserts, "The Universe is the externalization of the soul" (1844/1981, p. 248) and "The book of Nature is the book of Fate" (1860/1981, p. 354). The Transcendentalists were of the first contemporary intellectuals to fully appreciate the link between psychology and ecology. For the Greeks, their very religion was rooted in the earth.

The gods were not transcendental beings beyond the earth but were in actuality the forces operating in everyday life. Deities were earthly manifestations. Psychologists have ignored this body of work and treated it as the purview of the humanities. However, a careful reading of Transcendentalists, including Emerson and the Greek poets, reveals a wealth of psychological insights, as Nietzsche, for one, recognized. As a result of their investigations, we could benefit by rooting our psychology in the Earth and its ecology. The link between psychology, biology, and ecology can be strengthened and the lines between these fields more clearly delineated. Any immediate tendency to divide the fields leads to cul-de-sacs in all of them and the hidden hand of the Moirae remains un-knowable.

We have thus far related the Moirae to biology and ecology because it is vitally important that we retain the perspective that the Moirae are reality itself. However, our focus is primarily on the *psychological* interpretation of this existence. Perhaps future researchers will examine in greater depth the important conjunction between human consciousness and reality itself in relation to the Moirae.

2. Personal Future Unconscious

The Moirae are manifested psychologically through our personal future unconscious. Each person is a destiny manifested at the unconscious level. Our behavior and cognition are shaped by a teleology of which we are only intuitively aware. Contemporary psychological research provides many examples of our personal future unconscious. However, the research is superficial and is not derived from a larger meta-theoretical perspective. We will therefore be better able to perceive how such research relates to larger patterns through our discussion of the Moirae.

The Moirae most obviously determine our demographic fate in life. In other words, our historical, geographical, socio-economic, and familial situations are circumstances most directly influenced by the Moirae. Take note that, although all social scientists believe that the individual's situation at birth is extremely important, no one is able to explain why I was born, for example, in 1967, in Pittsburgh, into a white, middle-class, blue-collar household. Every psychologist would acknowledge that my child development was unique because my closest sibling in age is 18 years older. However, would any psychologist attempt to explain why I was born at all? It is here in this realm that social scientists are most likely to throw up their hands and assert "It is fate!" or "It is chance!"

The Moirae not only lay the demographic foundation for our lives but they also shape our biological and personality development. Later chapters will investigate the role of physiological and genetic factors, but suffice it to say here, that most social science research shows a strong correlation between early biological variables and personality. However, as we grow, the Moirae become more elastic, allowing us to stretch the boundaries of our personality and to individualize our destiny. After all, as I tell my classes, we all know what an extravert is, but how many of us know two people who are identical in their extraversion?

At the same time, we are unconsciously being pulled toward particular growth patterns. We feel drawn to particular behaviors that define our very being. How many people do we know who engage repeatedly in detrimental behavior and seem incapable of stopping? For example, most addictive behaviors become increasingly stronger over time. A mistake that we find in the psychological literature is that we too often look to the *past* as an explanation for behavior. This is indeed baffling, in that so few psychological variables highly correlate with addiction. However, phenomenologically, almost all addicts report being drawn *toward* particular behaviors. In other words, addicts are often incapable of explaining why they engage in a behavior that they logically realize is self-defeating; nevertheless they obsessively imagine, dream, and plan drug-related activity. In other words, they are drawn unconsciously toward the drug use, alcohol, smoking, gambling, or overeating. Until they are schooled in the language of treatment and recovery, few addicts report experiences consistent with the theories of addiction. We can extend this argument to aggressive behavior where individuals are drawn to violence, athletic competition where players feel compelled to win, or to altruistic behavior where the person hears a "calling" to help.

In contemporary psychology, the area of research and theory development most consistent with the idea of a personal future unconscious is narrative psychology. Narrative psychology attempts to explain personality by characterizing the person as a storyteller whereby each individual possesses a mind which elaborates and creates a life story. Tales contain settings and characters and conform to the basic storytelling elements. For example, Dan McAdams (1999) has extended Erikson's ideas about identity development in order to conceptualize the self as a life story that integrates the events of a person's life into particular thematic lines. Some theorists have gone further and categorized the types of stories generated into taxonomies such as reform narratives, commitment stories, stability narratives, and so forth.

These developments in personality theory are not revolutionary. They evolve from a historical foundation of other psychologists, philosophers, writers, and artists who have explored and expressed ideas regarding human existence. Joseph Campbell (1949) wrote extensively about the universality of the hero myth through history. The story of the hero's separation, initiation, and return is apparent in Greek mythology, the story of Jesus, in literature, and epic films such as Star Wars. Jean-Paul Sartre (1965) configured the self as a "true novel," that is, a retrospective myth a person creates to establish order out of the mystery of existence. Each "true novel" contains a central tenet reflecting issues within each person's historical period of development. Others who have contributed to this narrative mode of understanding include Jerome Bruner, Erik Erikson, Carl Jung, David Elkind, Silvan Tomkins, Henry Murray, Alfred Adler, Fyodor Dostoyevsky, Northrop Frye, and even Sigmund Freud (McAdams, 2001). This list is far from exhaustive since it includes only a sampling of the influential individuals sympathetic to a narrative conceptualization of the person from approximately 1860.

However, a bias against fatalism is again prevalent in this area of research. Rather than to interpret narrative research as the expressive vehicle of a pre-existing narrative structure present within the life structure from birth, psychologists have decided that these stories are generated after the events take place. Why is this assumption made? The only plausible reason is that this assumption fits into the prevailing world view. However, such a decision does not change the fact that, since ancient Greece, people have believed in predeterminism and that, by living life, their own personal narratives unfold.

Of all narrative theorists, those with a psychoanalytic orientation are most amenable to an acceptance of fatalism. The works of Carl Jung and Joseph Campbell rest on the concepts of archetypes and a collective unconscious. The collective unconscious is an archaic repository of remnants from our evolutionary past; it is our shared human memory, albeit the most inaccessible layer of the human psyche. The collective unconscious is presumed to contain archetypes that are biological predispositions (or templates) that facilitate the interpretation of human experience. Archetypes are not inherited memories, but rather are predispositions that shape how we interpret events, or in contemporary narrative theory, how we tell stories. A classic example that Jung (1951/1971) cites is "the shadow." This is the "dark side" of our personality that embodies our primal desires. We see this archetype manifested in our cultural views, for example, of Satan, aliens, and Hitler, and is typically projected onto enemies.

Erik Erikson (1980) also implicitly adopts an unconscious fatalism through his eight stages of human development. He notes that each individual must pass through a stage corresponding to a particular chronological age. In other words, Erikson inextricably links our biology with our personality and social development. For example, the infant must first establish a sense of trust about the world in order to achieve autonomy, industry, and so forth. Each stage provides us with a crisis rooted in our chronological age. In a sense, we are predestined to encounter this crisis. Furthermore, Erikson's theory is rooted in what he calls the epigenetic principle. He states ". . . that anything that grows has a *ground plan*, and that out of this ground plan the *parts* arise, each part having its *time* of ascendancy, until all parts have arisen to form a *functioning whole*." We can clearly see that this statement is consistent with a teleological, unconscious fatalism. The implications of this revolutionary statement have not yet been explored, despite that psychology textbooks contain numerous references to Erikson's theory.

The genetically-transferred universal archetypes of Jung and Erikson's stages are actualized at the level of the individual, therefore psychological theorists should next ask why these narrative forms, archetypes, and universal stages exist within us. If they do not exist to guide us and help us form a coherent pattern to our lives, why are they here? By conceptualizing narratives, archetypes, and stages as the Moirae—manifestations of our personal future unconscious drawing us toward our destiny—we may then attain a psychological concept with real *meaning*. Archetypes are not an evolutionary repository; instead, they are, I would argue, the very foundation of human existence which pulls us toward the future.

3. Genetic Basis of the Moirae

The Moirae are materially transmitted from the universe, the earth, and nature to us via our genetic structures. Some of the Moirae appear as physical attributes (e.g., sex, hair color, and body structure), while others are experienced psychologically or spiritually. However, their roots lie in our very "material" essence: our biology. Biological scientists do not always explain phenomena in the most poetic manner. This is unfortunate, since any artist or writer who fully appreciates biology can feel the ethereal beauty of the physical and biological world. Examples of poetical expression of the notion of human limitations abound in Greek myth and poetry, where the forces of the world are not lamented but are instead celebrated. Life is sacred and excellence is pursued because of a fatalistic attitude toward life and especially, death.

The genetic predestination discussed here is typically a "soft predestination"; variations of it have already been accepted by psychologists, but only within the paradigm of past causality. After all, the environmental determinism of stimulus-response psychology or the unconscious forces Freud posits are highly deterministic; these forces propel us into the future. However, the teleological idea of a "genetic future causation" in psychology, or forces which pull the individual into the future, have not even begun to be addressed. Quantum physics and chaos theory have shown that "b" can cause "a" at the microscopic level. In other words, the effect precedes the cause. Why can this not be true for human personality? We see evidence from genetic research which indicates archetypal patterns in the future; these archetypal patterns begin as the genetic structure of the person, and later blossom into the future personal unconscious. The collective unconscious of humanity "holds" common patterns among human beings for future life courses, shaping the paths of our relationships, our career choices, our interests and hobbies, our health, and even our deaths. Our genetic structure at birth shapes our personal unconscious, which is where the future lies. Our future is not *dictated* by genes or the personal unconscious; however, our behavior and cognition are shaped by it. This is not a Freudian unconscious laden exclusively with Oedipal conflicts, and sexual and aggressive urges, although these factors are undoubtedly important. The Moirae is an unconscious filled with the future.

Psychoanalysis and evolutionary psychology are two fields within psychology that can be interpreted from this perspective. We will fully explore these connections in chapter six.

4. Possession: The Future Unconscious Seizes Us

At times the Moirae seem phenomenologically to possess us and control our behavior. The behavior in which we engage may be irrational and in contraposition to our conscious plans, yet we continue the behavior. Let us consider the overweight person who is inevitably drawn from one fad diet to another. Education seems to make little difference in the person's behavior and he or she may fully acknowledge what every nutritional expert knows: The way to lose weight is to exercise regularly, reduce fat and caloric intake, and increase fruit and vegetable consumption. Still, the person seems incapable of adopting this plan. The donut and couch appeal to them in a way that the slender, athletic person cannot understand.

Moreover, the phenomenon of rage, an expression of many violent criminals, is anathema to those who do not feel surges of physical aggression. A trigger in the person blinds all rationality and he or she is sucked into an escalating level of violence. Most humans, however, have probably experienced rage at some point in their lives. As noted by Hatab (1990), the sense of an extra-human force that seizes our thought processes was also well-understood among the Greeks. Whether it is genius, heroism, or rage, the idea that an extra-human force can "seize us," is a prevalent concept across human history and culture.

Ultimately, a violent person is prepared to act in moments of intense aggressive situations. Psychological research has shown that aggressive people are drawn to violent movies, video games, and fantasies which provide them with cognitive scripts and modeled behaviors for enacting their aggressive impulses (see Geen & Donnerstein, 1998 for a review). When the violent person is seized by rage, destiny is fulfilled, because a cultural repository of thoughts and actions is available.

5. Cycles

The Moirae are manifested in our lives in accordance with cyclical patterns. The best examples involve the biological functions: sleeping, eating, etc. which all occur in daily cycles. We can exert our will by staying up late, rising early, or skipping a meal, but the Moirae demand that we pay for such transgressions. We also observe cyclical behavior and life patterns on a weekly level, with church on Sunday, work Monday through Friday, soccer on Wednesday. Years too are structured cyclically, given our acknowledgment of holidays, vacations, seasonal sports, academic years, and birthdays. Interestingly, Earth, nature, and the universe also operate in cyclical patterns, once again illustrating humanity's tie to the universe through the Moirae. A more detailed analysis of the cyclical nature of our being and its tie to the universe will be discussed in chapters three and four.

6. Freedom

A final characteristic of the Moirae important to our discussion here concerns the nature of human freedom. Although it may sound paradoxical, Sartre stated that "Man is condemned to be free." Humans have grappled with the issue of free will and determinism across the ages. We value freedom on the one hand with a deep conviction, but we can also shun it like an unwanted stepchild, either because it is too difficult or because we undervalue it. Psychology has never adequately addressed the issue. As researchers and theorists, we typically behave like determinists; however, at the personal level we readily acknowledge human free will. At first glance, the ideas presented in this book seem to be yet another deterministic enterprise, albeit from a new angle. Upon closer examination, however, the reader will notice that the meta-theoretical framework presented here provides, to date, one of the most detailed explanations of the relationship between free will and determinism in psychology. As a result, an approach using the Moirae details explicitly the very important role of free will in our lives. Other psychological theories ignore the issue, thereby devaluing it. It is ironic that, highlighting the significance of free will within psychology may require a theorist who is interested in fate.

We will therefore explore it fully in chapter five. However, at this point we need to emphasize that the Moirae provide a framework for our lives. They do not dictate our precise, everyday behaviors, and within this framework we make important decisions that alter our lives. There are some issues, however, which can never be changed or are unlikely to be changed. A person born with Down's syndrome is destined to face issues in life that others will never encounter. Possessing the genetic structure to be seven feet tall and being born in America orients one in particular directions that others will not be able to pursue.

Before we continue with a more precise description of the Moirae's cyclical nature and explore the role of free will, let us illustrate two concrete manifestations of the Moirae. The first is death, which is the ultimate Moirae. Death provides the greatest example of the relationship between determinism and free will. Our destiny of death, and an awareness of it, provides us with vitality for life, beauty, and excellence. A resignation to the certainty death, which we all must accept, compels us to value life greatly. Knowledge of death provides a circumscribed perimeter within which we make sacred choices in a temporal world.

An Example: Death, The Ultimate Moirae

A sense of gravity in our lives guides us to our eventual destination, the black hole of human existence, death. The phenomenon of death is a wonderful exemplar of a Moirae because it is personal yet universal. Our death is the most powerful psychological force guiding us along our life path; however, it is also a force which destroys plants, animals, planets, universes, and even ideas. Death preexists, as an unconscious, archetypal structure, ubiquitous in nature while also continuously manifested at a material level. Inherent in the cycle of life, death is also the food of life. On a personal level death provides life with meaning and structure. Our genetic code demands that we die, and it is known to shape the nature and timing of death. At a societal level (common among other Moirae), we tend to personify death; arguably, the most common personification of death in our culture is the "Grim Reaper." A figure cloaked in black; tall, dark, menacing, and yielding a seemingly necromantic walking stick. We also find slightly disguised permutations of the grim reaper in our contemporary entertainment (e.g., Darth Vader from Star Wars and Sauron from The Lord of the Rings).

Death is certainly a powerful force in our personal lives. According to Freud (1920/1995), we possess a death instinct which is the human, unconscious goal to return to the inorganic world. More commonly, however, this unconscious desire is directed outward onto others resulting in aggression. Existential philosophers and psychologists have illustrated how the temporal nature of our being compels us to live our lives in meaningful ways. Heidegger (1953/1996) posits whether Da-sein (i.e., being, life) is ever complete without death. He alludes to whether "being" resembles an unripe fruit but without the phenomenon of death. Furthermore, he questions if death truly signifies the end of being. He concludes that,

> In death, Da-sein is neither fulfilled nor does it simply disappear; it has not become finished or completely available as something at hand. Rather, just as Da-sein constantly already is its not-yet as long as it is, it also always already is its end. The ending that we have in view when we speak of death, does not signify a being-at-an-end of Da-sein, but rather a *being toward the end* of this being. Death is a way to be that Da-sein takes over as soon as it is. . . . In the broadest sense, death is a phenomenon of life (pp. 228–9).

In a fatalistic framework, the Moirae calls us toward fulfillment in death, but death itself is not completeness. Our destiny of death urges us to become what one truly is. Similarly, Sartre (1943/1983) reminds us that, "Death reunites us with ourselves. Eternity has changed us into ourselves. At the moment of death we *are*. . . ."(p. 169).

In other words, death changes us from a living consciousness into an object where we become our past. However, we must take care not to identify ourselves with our past as we travel along life's journey. In so doing we remain trapped within what Sartre calls "bad faith," by treating ourselves as objects (a "being-in-itself").

With the exception of Freud, these theorists have focused on how we avoid death itself as well as thoughts relating to death. The value of this approach is undeniable. However, we should also consider that we may unconsciously *desire* death, not just avoid it. Many self-destructive behaviors such as addictions can be viewed in this light. Often, though, the Moirae's effects are subtle. A wonderful example of how we are unconsciously drawn to death is illustrated in a classic study by Kastenbaum and Briscoe (1975), who observed 125 individuals crossing a street corner and interviewed those who engaged in the riskiest and the safest behaviors. The "risky" crossers (i.e., those who crossed in the middle of the block, did not check for traffic, etc.) described themselves as high-risk drivers, were four times more likely to have contemplated or attempted suicide than were the "safe" pedestrians, and indicated greater levels of frustration with life. The "chance" of encountering death is obviously much higher for the "risky" crossers, and is apparently related to their emotional and attitudinal approach to life in general.

The previous study shows how our future death may influence us in subtle ways. However, our future death can often seize us and completely dominate our being. I have labeled this phenomenon "possession" because the term best communicates how the Moirae rises to assume control over us. In other words, our future unconscious seizes and overpowers us.

Let us discuss two emotional states related to death that illustrate this principle. The first is the emotional state of grief. Grief is characterized by an overwhelming sense of sadness and loss. More importantly, we find that grief influences all aspects in one's life (see Averill & Nunley, 1993). Our physical body is altered and disturbances occur in sleep patterns, appetite, energy levels, and brain neurotransmitters. Our cognition, attitudes, and emotional state dramatically change. Social relationships are altered by the death of a loved one. Furthermore, grief appears to be a universal response to death. In other words, the "chance" event of death affects all human beings at every level of their existence; the death of a loved one reminds us of our own mortality and dramatically illustrates the temporal nature of life. Furthermore, the death of those most similar to us evokes the most profound sense of grief. The death of a close pet for example does not provoke the same emotional response as the death of a family member. Our grief is at least partially a response to our own future death. The Moirae seizes us and dominates our future actions for months, and sometimes years, after the event.

Secondly, depression is also a state of hopelessness and loss which is characterized by suicidal ideation and repeated thoughts of death. Depression and death are linked not only clinically, but also in art, literature, and music. Anyone familiar with the stories of Edgar Allen Poe can attest to the sometimes eloquent manner in which authors articulate the link between depression and death. Depression moreover is at least partially determined by our genetic constitution (Gershon, Berrettini, Nurnberger & Goldin, 1989), and similar to grief, can influence every level of our existence from the physical state to social relationships. Individuals with depression can be, arguably, seized by the Moirae of death. Their personal, future unconscious has seized control of the person's being, haunting it with loss and hopelessness.

The cyclical nature of the Moirae is also exemplified by the phenomenon of death. On a material level, death feeds life. All forms of life depend on the death of plants and animals for survival. The circle of life depends on the physical decay of living beings. At the other end of the spectrum we can view death as a spiritual cycle. Reincarnation, rebirth, and the concept of an afterlife are central to most religions; Hinduism and Christianity provide illustrative examples of these concepts. Hindu beliefs indicate that humanity's place in the universe is defined through reincarnation, in which the goal is to escape the cycle of birth, death, and rebirth to reach a higher level of consciousness. Christianity provides us with an image of rebirth into a Platonic afterlife characterized by bliss and harmony, at least for those who have proven worthy. A wonderful example of the spiritual cycle taken from ancient Egyptian mythology is the image of the Phoenix: a bird that consumes itself in the fire of a funeral pyre and is reborn from its own ashes to live another cycle of years. The phoenix has also been thought to represent the sun (Cotterell, 1989). The daily journey of the sun represents the cycle of life and death. In each of these examples death is linked materially or spiritually to rebirth.

Finally, the horizon of death provides meaning for the sacred choices we make in a world where we measure time. The Moirae of death clarifies the role of freedom in our life. Viewed from one angle, death is the purest example of determinism. We all must die. Therefore, our very birth harkens the calling of our death. They are forever linked. However, the nature and timing of our death is often the result of free will. In complete contrast to a deterministic perspective, death is ultimate freedom. I could, for example, choose not to complete this sentence and instead end my very existence at this moment. I can also make subtle choices about the timing of my own death. The foods we eat and the activities in which we engage can typically prolong or shorten our lives. However, we may be fooled by this sense of freedom and control. The most loyal health advocate could in fact die momentarily from a heart attack, brain tumor, or a car accident. The inevitability of death poignantly demonstrates the unique freedom available to human beings. We will return to this issue in depth in chapter five.

A Second Example: Sex

Sexuality is comprised of what Freud (1920/1995) labeled the libido, or life instinct. It is the psychic force that propels us toward survival and reproduction. The libido can be invested in an activity, in God, or even in the self. However, we most often observe that the "object choice" of the libido is another person. Human sexuality is the text that the libido authors, and so we find that six characteristics of the Moirae are also manifested in human sexuality. Nature reveals itself in the bipolar nature of male and female, in for example, such distinctions in the plant, animal, and human aspects of life. Sexuality is deeply rooted in our biological existence but it is also rooted psychologically at the unconscious and conscious levels and forms the cultural patterns of our lives. The tension between male and female that gives rise to the vitality of life is also found in mythology. Greek mythology divides the world into the feminine, dark, passionate underworld of the Titans, and the masculine, intelligent, beauty of the Olympian gods. However, as Hatab (1990) states, ". . . such a distinction does not refer primarily to sexual gender but rather to a kind of cosmic duality" (p. 56). The Greeks found themselves positioned between these two worlds of ". . . passion and moderation, chaos and order, animal drives and culture, malevolence and benevolence, death and life" (p. 56). Tension between conceptually polar opposites helps shape the dynamism and vitality within ourselves and among us in society.

Our personal future unconscious beckons us at the moment of conception. At that moment a chief, defining characteristic of our personality and life pattern is partially determined: our gender. Little does the fetus realize that the presence of an XY or XX pattern in his or her genetic structure dictates the future of this person regardless of culture, historical period, geographical region, etc. (all of which are also determined by the Moirae) into which they are hurled. The sex of an infant has always carried important implications regarding behavior, cognition, personality, and social roles, but none of us recalls choosing such an important variant in our lives. Nor can psychologists indicate why I am male and not female in any existentially, meaningful sense. I simply am male and science proceeds from this fact.

As psychoanalysis and evolutionary psychology have shown, my gender will have profound implications on my unconscious life and the social behaviors in which I engage. We know that sex is influenced (almost exclusively) by genetic structure. The physical effects of genes first form in the uterus, creating the prenatal environment through the release of specific hormones. At birth my physical characteristics, for example, then create a social environment that influences my psychological development: was I to be placed in a blue room with footballs or a pink room with dolls? When I reach age three, gender becomes the key social component of my identity (Maccoby, 1988). This is true even if parents do not emphasize gender-specific roles, and despite the fact that young children do not necessarily make a connection between the defining physical characteristics of gender (i.e., XY and penis, or XX and vagina) and the social category of gender. Developmental psychologists and educators unequivocally agree that gender is central to identity by the time we reach the pre-school years.

Once we enter puberty, the Moirae become evident on a physical level in relation to psychological and social changes. Again the connection is clear, we are born with a genetic structure that reveals itself physically and then psychologically. In the case of puberty, our genetic personal, future unconscious has *pulled us* to the experiences and changes of adolescence. The Moirae operate by physically changing our bodies and psychologically altering our unconscious, *pulling us* toward a future of which we are as unaware as was the fetus. Throughout adolescence our gender shapes us in new ways. Earlier it drew us toward certain friends, particular toys, and activities. Now it begins to shape our attitudes, sexual behavior, and career choices.

As we emerge into young, middle, and late adulthood, sex again powerfully shapes our behavior and cognition. I need not step on each stone of the life path in order to illustrate the power of sexuality in our lives. Anyone familiar with the research literature of development and personality psychology can find a veritable gold mine of examples to illustrate the impact of sex.

The critic may stop me at this point and argue that gender is socially constructed and that the behavior of men and women is historically and culturally contingent; this assertion is indeed valid. Undoubtedly, humans have chosen this physical difference and culturally-prescribed acceptable behaviors and cognitions. However, I must also note that such an insightful observation is irrelevant to the present analysis. Irrespective of which culture or historical period a person is born into, *being male or female is still central to the life path.* Gender roles are socially constructed (even the very idea of gender is a human construction). However, cultures throughout the history of humankind have decided that gender is an important aspect of existence. Furthermore, the critic's astute observation illustrates the broad-based power of the Moirae: history and culture are also material manifestations of the Moirae! We are cast not only into our sex but also into the culture and time period which will define what sex as a physical attribute means for each person; that is, how gender is socially constructed.

The Moirae of sex can also "seize" or possess us, and it too expresses itself cyclically. For some, the physical need for sex is overpowering, especially when one deviates from one's own "normal" sex cycle. The desire to procreate dominates the lives of many young couples, while the reproductive physiology of women is one of the finest examples of the physiological and psychological importance of cycles in human lives. Conversely, the darker side of the possessive nature of sex is rape: an act of hate and aggression. However, the very definition of rape is contingent upon the sexual act: the rapist is possessed with the need for sexual expression and violence is the path.

Finally, although sexuality is genetically-based and universal, we also see the expression of free will within it. A life of celibacy or promiscuity can be chosen. Sex can be used for pleasure, money, or as the articulation of love. We can observe how some paths along the mountainside of life appear to be wide and clear while others are precarious and entangled with brush and undergrowth. But here again we see human free will paradoxically manifested within the confines of a powerful determinant.

Free will can also be expressed more subtly within the realm of gender and sex. On a cognitive level, gender is a schema or a category used to comprehend the social world. For philosophers such as Ludwig Wittgenstein and William James and many contemporary cognitive psychologists, the fundamental act of cognition is categorization. Wittgenstein (1953) discusses the notion of "family resemblance" in relation to our propensity to categorize. Most people assume that all members of a category share some defining feature (e.g., birds fly) however, this isn't the case (e.g., penguins). "The family resemblance concept asserts that a category does not have to have a defining feature that all members share. Instead, there can be a set of features that is distributed across the category members, with no single feature essential for category inclusion" (Thorne & Henley, 2005, p. 550).

What role does free will play in our cognitive categorizations of gender? We construct and choose the "family resemblance" for gender. Let me relate a personal example. My son age five and I were looking through an illustrated anatomy manual learning about the circulatory and digestive systems when a discussion of sex differences arose. While viewing the anatomically-correct nude figures, my son noted which figures were "boys" and which were "girls." I asked him how he "knew" some were boys and some were girls. He did not mention the presence of a penis or a vagina as most adults would (yes reader, he is familiar with those words). Instead, he listed a variety of disparate characteristics (e.g., woman with long hair, man had dark skin) and no essential, defining characteristics. I challenged him on some of these characteristics (e.g., Can't a man have long hair?), to no avail. His response was similar to a former Supreme Court Justice who, when asked to define pornography, claimed that he could not define it, but that he knew it when he saw it. My son's categorization of sex is closer to the truth than our typical genetic or biological definitions. Gender is a malleable, freedom-laden concept whose meaning is contingent upon many other culturally-defined terms and ideas (e.g., cross-dressing, sex changes, homosexuality, bisexuality, and trans-sexuality). There are many ways that, through acts of freedom, such powerful Moirae as sex can be defined.

Now that I have provided two concrete examples of how the Moirae are revealed, it would be more fruitful for us to return to a discussion of important characteristics such as the cyclical nature of the fates and the role of free will.

Part Two: Cycles

Chapter 3

Daily Drumbeats: The Rhythms of Life

"Anatomy is destiny." –Sigmund Freud (1924/1995, p. 665)

According to the ancients, the Moirae can become clear to the eye or mind in the geometric form of the "circle." They regarded the circle as a symbol of unity and as alpha and omega. The circle is also a symbolic form of rhythm. It is perfection; a cycle whereby our journey begins and ends at the same point. The circle is a Platonic representation of the cyclical nature of life and the Moirae. The cyclical rhythm of life is inextricably grounded in biological processes. Everything, from our solar system to the structure of the atom, is cyclical in nature. We can observe the circle of the Moirae in the seasons, the life cycles of animals, and in life itself.

To every thing there is a season,
and a time to every purpose under heaven;
A time to be born, and a time to die;
a time to plant, and a time to pluck up that which is planted;
A time to kill, and a time to heal;
a time to break down, and a time to build up;
A time to weep, and a time to laugh;
a time to mourn, and a time to dance;
A time to cast away stones,
and a time to gather stones together;
a time to embrace, and a time to refrain from embracing;
A time to get, and a time to lose;
a time to keep, and a time to cast away;
A time to rend, and a time to sew;
a time to keep silence, and a time to speak;
A time to love, and a time to hate;
a time of war, and a time of peace.

The planet Saturn was viewed as the symbol of perfection because of its rings. The mythological serpent forms a circle as it consumes its own tail. The beautiful Mandalas of the East and the sand paintings of the Navajo Indians include the circle. Thoreau's *Walden* (1854/1996) forms a literary circle ending with, ". . . but such is the character of that morrow which mere lapse of time can never make to dawn. The light which puts out our eyes is darkness to us. Only that day dawns to which we are awake. There is more day to dawn. The sun is but a morning star" (p. 323). The very foundation of music and poetry, moreover, is rhyme and meter.

We could dedicate many pages to discussion on the rhythms of nature, other mythical aspects of the circle, or to the literary use of rhyme. However, the purpose of this free-form writing is to emphasize the ubiquity of the circle and highlight our primary concern, which is the existence of the Moirae within the realm of human psychology. Let us next examine how the Moirae of the circle is played out biologically, psychologically, spiritually, and socially at the human level.

Time-Governed Cycles

The root of our biological existence lies in cyclical replication. The generation of chromosomal structure and replication is the basis not only of our biological life but also of ritual. Each chromosome is comprised of DNA, a double-helix molecule where replication drives cell division. The divisional process of replication produces the random variation of genetic expression central to the diversity of life and in turn drives the evolutionary process of natural selection. The subsequent genetic diversity produced through chromosomal replication operates according to a cyclical, repetitive chemical pattern, thus yielding planetary life and consciousness.

Biological existence is infused with the Moirae of the circle. The brain's electrical activity, the heartbeat, breath, digestion, hormonal secretions, and other basic physiological functions, operate in an oscillating fashion. These "drumbeats of life" are essential to our existence. Perhaps the most interesting of these rhythms function in an approximate 24-hour "circadian" cycle. These daily cycles operate in an array of organisms at the biochemical, physiological, and behavioral levels, and many are regulated—not by environmental forces—but by internal cues. For instance, most animals function according to a basic rest-activity cycle. Animals will follow a specified activity pattern even when environmental cyclical patterns such as light are held constant. However, these environmental stimuli often act altogether as zeitgeber, or time givers, which synchronize our internal rhythms. A caged rat in a laboratory environment may run in its wheel all night and sleep during the day, despite that the lab light emits a uniform intensity of illumination throughout the 24-hour period.

The neural metronome that coordinates these circadian rhythms is situated in the hypothalamus of the brain. Specifically, researchers have identified the suprachiasmatic nucleus (SCN) as the primary coordinator of daily rhythms. Just as a flywheel, pendulum, or quartz crystal can serve to parse time into discrete units for clocks, the SCN must have a time base. Physiological research has not provided definitive evidence regarding this base, but the leading hypothesis indicates that the synthesis of proteins and the negative feedback loop associated with the generation and dissipation of proteins serves to parse time for the neurons. Furthermore, we find that the SCN is also affected by light variations in the environment through neural connections to the visual system. By incorporating this information, the SCN controls drinking, eating, sleeping, and hormonal secretion through other neural projections in the brain.

Let us explore an essential area of behavior related to circadian rhythms. The Moirae of the circle are observed in our daily sleep cycles. By the time we reach age 60 most of us will have spent 20 years sleeping (Rosenzweig & Leiman, 1989). We are drawn to sleep, we can postpone it or temporarily abandon it, but we cannot escape its lure. The evidence is clear; we must sleep or suffer dire consequences. The nature of each night's sleep can vary depending on age, occupation, and stress levels; however, the basic cycles remain the same for everyone. During the first 90 minutes of sleep we gradually move from a state of wakefulness to deep rest. Stage 1 is characterized as the transition to true sleep as the eyes dart about and brain waves begin to alter (i.e., "delta" waves, 3.5-7.5Hz, appear on an EEG). After about 10 minutes we enter stage 2 where we see a decreased receptivity to external stimuli and the emergence of "sleep spindles" (12-14Hz waves) on an EEG. Stages 3 and 4 begin about 30 minutes after the onset of sleep and are characterized by high-amplitude "delta" waves (< 3.5Hz) where stage 3 sleep contains 20-50% delta waves and stage 4 contains more than 50% (Carlson, 1991).

After approximately 90 minutes of sleep, our eyes begin to dart back and forth rapidly, our muscles relax completely, brain wave activity now becomes erratic, and most importantly, we begin to dream. This stage is known as REM sleep (rapid eye movement). Researchers have concluded that this is the most important sleep stage. The onset of REM begins due to the internal "alarm clock" (Carlson, 1991). Learning, memory, muscle restoration, and psychological disorders are contingent upon REM sleep. Psychoanalytic theorists have found REM sleep to be central to their theorizing about the unconscious. Since publication of Freud's (1899/2006) *The Interpretation of Dreams*, psychoanalysts have regarded dreams as a reservoir of unconscious desires, brimming with symbolic meaning. For Freudian theorists, the symbolism involves personal sexual and/or aggressive themes, whereas for Jungians, archetypal images from the collective unconscious emerge within a person's dreamscape. Despite the supposed link between the unconscious and dreaming, a systematic method of interpretation of dream symbols has never been fully developed. Therefore, most scientifically-oriented psychologists do not recognize the value of dream symbolism. However, almost any psychologists will acknowledge that dreaming relates to the resolution of personal issues and problems. It thus seems reasonable to assume that the unconscious plays a role in our dreams.

The sleep cycle influences learning, memory, stress levels, hormonal secretions, and neurochemical activity. We also have discovered that many psychological disorders, including depression, are directly associated with malfunctions and interruptions in our circadian rhythms. Therefore, our daily circle is the result of endogenous biological mechanisms that propel us through the day.

Circadian (daily) rhythms have been most frequently studied in humans. However, we also find our biology and psychology rooted in the monthly lunar cycle. Females normally experience a physiological and psychological phenomenon called the menstrual cycle each month; it is governed by the hormonal secretions of the pituitary gland and ovaries. (There is also evidence that males may be influenced by a women's cycle and that he himself may also experience slight variations in hormonal levels according to a monthly cycle.) Hormonal changes influence us not only biologically but also psychologically and emotionally. The female's monthly cycle is the basis for reproduction, so it logically follows that human conception is rooted in the lunar cycle. We again find ourselves embedded in a cosmic, biological circle that is crucial for human life.

Finally, we note that it is becoming increasingly accepted that our behavior is linked to our planet's yearly rotation around the sun, what neuroscientists call "circannual rhythms." It is well-known that, for many animals the seasons are key indicators of activity, primarily due to environmental factors like food availability. Although we do not share an annual hibernation cycle with some of our fellow animals (despite its lure), we do find mounting evidence that humans are psychologically influenced by circannual rhythms, of which the most obvious example is Seasonal Affective Disorder (SAD). Other mood problems such as bipolar disorder are also characterized by cyclical mood patterns, but SAD is directly related to the seasonal pattern. Serious depressive episodes occur during the winter months, allegedly due to darker days, triggering hormonal changes, such as melatonin, in the body. Research suggests that, for some who suffer from SAD, the summer is a time of elation and activity, which parallels the cycles of bipolar disorder. In fact, researchers Goodwin, Wirz-Justice, and Wehr (1982) claim that all mood disorders are caused by disturbances in circadian rhythms. Other behaviors which are perhaps related to SAD, are unique to the winter season; at this time many individuals experience increased consumption of carbohydrates, weight gain, lethargy, and the "winter blahs." Finally, we observe that when many Northerners retire, they spend the winter months in places like Florida and Arizona, thus mimicking the migration patterns of other animals.

The Moirae of the circle seizes us at night calling us to a world of biological restoration and resolution of unconscious conflicts. It wakes us in the morning, guiding us to periods of rest and activity where we are free to pursue our interests within a biological framework. Our biology and unconscious are synchronous with the Earth's rotation, the sunrise and sunset. Each month and year we reenact ritualistic patterns of emotion, cognition, and behaviors in tune with the Moon's orbit around the earth, the Earth's orbit around the sun, rooted in the structure of the solar system. Our daily, monthly, and yearly choices are thus not only embedded in the neurochemical ground of human biology but also in the astronomical fabric of the universe.

Life Pattern Cycles

We have seen how our lives interweave with nature in the short-term. However, we also find ritualistic patterns over the long-term. An examination of every individual life would reveal cyclical patterns of behavior occurring over long time periods. I present four examples currently of interest to many psychologists as well as the wider public. They include research on drug/alcohol abuse, aggression, religious practice, and delay of gratification.

Drug and Alcohol Abuse

Anyone familiar with the treatment of drug and alcohol abuse knows that the foremost problem is relapse. Invariably all addicts return to their drug of choice. This is not only borne out by the "recidivism" rates of clinics and programs but also for those who attempt to quit on their own. Addicts find themselves ritualistically drawn back to the drug for myriad reasons: from loose associations (e.g., walking by a bar) to stressful, emotional events. The relapse cycle is the rule rather than the exception. An addict may begin using the drug of choice for many reasons including stress reduction, peer acceptance, or simply to get high. However, as many researchers have discovered, an addict's reasons for continued abuse can change over time. For example, Solomon (1977) has advanced an important theory explaining drug addiction, called opponent process theory. According to this theory, addiction is part of the biological mechanism of homeostasis, that is, the body's natural tendency to maintain biological equilibrium. Homeostasis operates according to a set point and feedback loop similar to a thermometer. Open a window on a cold winter's day, the room temperature drops, and the furnace initiates the process of moving the room temperature back to its set point. The body also uses the opponent process; one set of mechanisms moves us away from our set point, and another returns us to it. The process that restores our equilibrium strengthens over time while the initial process weakens. For example, a first-time heroin user experiences extreme euphoria and minimal consequence for the return to equilibrium. However, a hard core addict experiences little euphoria but grave consequences in the return to equilibrium. Those who imbibe alcohol can recall that, when young, they felt refreshed the morning after a night of excessive jubilation. However, as the years pass, most people choose to refrain from excessive intake, knowing the severe penalty to be paid the following day. The lesson is that, with repeated exposure to any drug, the euphoric, or initial phase away from our set point becomes weaker while our recovery, or restoring process lengthens and intensifies. In effect, a pervasive social problem has ritualistic tendencies rooted biologically in the process of homeostasis.

Finally, we also find similar patterns of behavior in other forms of "addictive" behaviors such as gambling and eating disorders. In fact, this pattern is so common among psychological disorders in general (including obsessive-compulsive disorder, bipolar disorder, and SADs) that it proves illuminating to conceptualize these disorders as maladaptive ritualistic behaviors. By so doing, we more closely see their relationship to "normal" human activities. A true paradigm shift would occur in the area of abnormal psychology if we were to adopt the cycle of the Moirae to explain the etiology of maladaptive behaviors and their treatment.

Aggression and Sadism

Aggression is a social problem that affects many individuals and families. We observe that forms of violence are recurrent and cyclical in nature including war, torture, rape, and domestic violence. Recidivism rates for violent offenses such as rape and physical aggregation are startlingly high. This presents a serious problem for criminologists and society. Domestic violence similarly concerns social scientists and the public. The classic description of domestic abuse is offered by Walker (1984). She argues that domestic violence occurs because of a "cycle" of abuse. In other words, spousal battering occurs in a cyclical pattern whereby the male will violently overreact to a minor transgression. This episode is typically followed by a period of reconciliation (or at least a reduction of tension) that serves as an intermittent positive reinforcement. Therefore, the couple operates in a cyclical pattern according to an intermittent, positive reinforcement schedule. Scully (1990) has found that many rapists describe their violence as habit-forming in the same terms as a drug-addiction. Finally, we find large-scale aggression such as war also seems to recur despite noble attempts to defuse international conflicts. Theorists such as Nietzsche, Freud, and Konrad Lorenz have argued for an instinctual basis for human aggression considering its near ubiquity.

Baumeister (1997) has applied the opponent-process theory discussed earlier to acts of sadism and violence. He notes that almost everyone's initial reaction to violence is negative. Sadists and abusers may initially be shocked, confused, and disgusted when they first hurt another person. However, because the human body strives to maintain its homeostasis as mentioned above, the opponent reaction to the violence is pleasure for the perpetrator. The first sadistic act is dominated by the negative experience, but if a person inflicts harm on repeat occasions, the negative reactions diminish and the positive responses strengthen with each subsequent violent act. Over time one learns to enjoy sadistic activity through the opponent process of returning the body to homeostasis.

Baumeister notes that this interpretation is consistent with comments from rapists, torturers, and serial murders who describe the "addictive" qualities of violence. However, the process differs from actual drug/alcohol addiction. For drug and alcohol addicts the pleasure is contained in the initial phase of becoming intoxicated, whereas recovering from an abusive session with a drug is negative. Violent behavior exhibits the opposite pattern where the initial phase is unpleasant and the "recovery" period is pleasant. This experience resembles that of sensation seekers who bungee jump, parachute, or hang-glide: they initially experience fear, but pleasure ensues from the experience of returning to homeostasis.

Religious and Cultural Rituals

Another important area of inquiry into cyclical life patterns involves an examination of how religious and cultural rituals relate to completing the circle of the Moirae. Religion has been a central factor in recent human history. An important component of religions is the ritualistic practice associated with spiritual belief. Joseph Campbell was one of the first scholars to note the consistency and importance of rituals across religions. Rituals are most often tied to myths. St. Augustine eloquently described the nature of God as a circle whose center was everywhere and circumference was nowhere. As Campbell (1988) emphasized, the ritual completes our circle to God: "the one great story of myth is that in the beginning we were united with the source, but that we were separated from it and now we must find a way to return." Ritualistic religious activities are designed to take us back to the start of our circle. Religious myths are the stories we tell, while religious rituals are the experience of spirituality.

As a practicing Roman Catholic, I am keenly aware of the role of ritual in religion, spirituality, and tradition. A Roman Catholic mass is a series of rituals within rituals with the entire mass serving an even larger ritualistic purpose. The mass is a reenactment of the Last Supper culminating in a symbolic ingestion of the body and blood of Christ. The sacrament of the Eucharist symbolizes a reunion with Christ and the completion of the circle. Within this framework are smaller rituals performed each Sunday in an identical sequence of events. For example, there is the Catholic tradition of reciting the Rosary, a circle of prayer beads, during the Mass. Finally, each "liturgical year" is structured around a series of celebrations, readings, and other religious events. The significance of ritual is not exclusive to Catholicism; it is central to most religions of the West and the East. These rituals provide meaning and a sense of unity to the believers. A transcendence of self into a larger reality and purpose is central to the ceremony. There is not only a sense of unity and oneness with fellow human beings but also with God. Obviously there are non-religious rituals that produce similar feelings. Patriotic holidays, ethnic celebrations, and family traditions produce similar feelings of unity.

We also find that ritual is central to the feelings of transcendence experienced by mystics and other religious devotees. In other words, rituals not only unify a congregation of believers, but they also are important to personal religious transformation. The very essence of prayer is ritualistic. Scholars have recently attempted to identify the biological significance of religious rituals. They claim that repetitive rhythmic stimulation alters brain functioning through the limbic and autonomic systems which can produce feelings of transcendence. Newberg, D'Aquili, and Rause (2001) show that, "All religious rituals, to be effective, must combine the essential content of a mythic story with the neurological reactions that bring the myth to life. The synthesis of these two elements (i.e., the sheer neurological function and the meaningful cultural content) is the true source of a ritual's power" (p. 95). Furthermore, these authors provide compelling scientific evidence for a link between ritual, biology, and transcendence. They believe that ritualistic behavior directly impacts the hypothalamus, limbic system, and autonomic nervous system that in turn influence the emotional experience of the participant.

Newberg et al. (2001) also present persuasive evidence for the evolutionary roots of ritual. The rhythm and repetition characteristic of human rituals is also found among animals in which ritual is key to their survival. Human beings bond together to form social groups that provide a common sense of purpose and identity. Human and other animals' rituals also facilitate communication, reduce aggression, maintain the social hierarchy, and are central to mating; by enhancing survival all these behaviors are evolutionarily adaptive to both individual and species.

Finally, our need to ritualize can also cultivate maladaptive behaviors. The best example is found in Obsessive-Compulsive Disorder (OCD). OCD is characterized by repetitive thoughts that produce anxiety and compulsions that dictate acts or thoughts that reduce the anxiety. Most obsessional ruminations result in elaborate ritualistic behaviors. These most often include hand-washing rituals, checking rituals, or "magical" rituals (repeating phrases or numbers). Those who suffer from OCD have an overarching desire to perform rituals that dominates everything and can destroy lives. Researchers have identified part of the etiology of OCD in our biology; those suffering from OCD show a higher metabolic rate in the orbital frontal cortex of the brain. The orbital frontal cortex generates many "normal," more "voluntary" ritualistic behaviors—compared to "involuntary" bodily drives (e.g., hunger) that are rooted in the hypothalamus. Interestingly, Freud explored the similarities between OCD and religious practices more than a century ago. He eventually reached the conclusion that all religion was a form of neurosis.

Delay of Gratification

An area of research less familiar to the general public yet directly related to the cyclical nature of our lives is Walter Mischel's studies in delay of gratification (e.g., see Mischel, 1983). The delay of gratification research is based on the process of self-regulation. We all learn to control our behaviors through internalized reinforcement and punishment systems. The origin of this self-regulatory system is an interaction of our biological needs and our early social learning experiences. In other words, our biological predisposition to behave in particular ways is shaped by internalizing standards, expectations, rules, and virtues. The bases for this internalized self-regulatory system are childhood rewards and punishments and modeling experiences.

One form of self-regulation in which children are forced to engage is delay of gratification. Children must learn to sacrifice the immediate reward for future treasure. Mischel has shown that our willingness to delay gratification is contingent upon the outcomes expected and how much we value these outcomes. If we learn that waiting will indeed produce a larger treasure that we value, we are better able as adults to delay gratification to a reasonable future. Often this ability to wait arises from our ability to engage in selective attention. Mischel found that children who can easily distract themselves from an immediate reward are better able to wait for the later reward. Early in life we learn this internal regulatory system through our own experiences and by observing others; we internalize a regulatory system based on trust in the environment and the promise of the future.

We learn from this research that each person brings particular competencies to each social situation. The research also indicates that we develop a personal work ethic based upon this self-regulatory system (Eisenberger & Shank, 1985). The ability to delay gratification is directly correlated with our willingness to expend considerable effort to obtain rewards. The ability to divert and control our attention, based on biology and childhood learning experiences, illustrates the freedom and constraint of the cyclical Moirae. Each day we bring with us our self-regulatory pattern to each situation: the workplace, relationship with our spouse, the disciplining of children, and the resolution of personal problems such as weight gain, unwillingness to exercise, and the smoking habit. The self-regulatory patterns in turn create many of the life patterns we discussed earlier. We may change spouse, career, and geographic residence, but we nevertheless bring the same self-regulatory system that has created the behavior cycles from our previous surroundings into our new situations.

Conclusions

What conclusions can we draw from our discussion in this chapter? First, rituals, cycles, and the circle are fundamental aspects of human existence. Second, these patterns also occur at all levels of the universe from the microscopic to the universal. Finally, human beings are intricately connected to this cyclical universe through our biological and genetic constitution. Our biological connection in turn shapes our culture, religion, daily behaviors, cognitions, and life patterns. The normal behaviors in which we engage and the psychological disorders to which we are subjected are cyclical in nature, as are patterns of the universe. Our cyclical nature has been identified by those outside the field of psychology, including Nietzsche, Emerson, and numerous ecological writers. However, psychologists have theoretically ignored the stature of the circle. As we ponder the circle and explore Nietzsche's philosophy, some readers will likely be reminded of the notion of "eternal recurrence"; this topic will be discussed in the next chapter.

Chapter 4

Eternity: Recurrence and Forms

Circulus Vitiosus Deus (A Vicious Circle Made God)
–Friedrich Nietzsche (1886/1966, p. 68)

The aim of the current chapter is to integrate two important philosophical strands of thought in order to deepen our understanding of the Moirae. To do this we will briefly examine the philosophies of Plato and Nietzsche and, in particular, integrate Plato's ideal forms and Nietzsche's ideas concerning eternal recurrence, with the notion of fatalism expressed through the Moirae. We will further show how the Moirae can enhance our understanding of the life of Jesus of Nazareth by using these two concepts. We will conclude with a discussion of how the ideas of Nietzsche, Plato, and the life of Jesus illustrate the tenets of an unconscious fatalism. In many ways our discussion and example will incorporate the issues already discussed as well as those challenging us in later chapters.

Plato's Eternal Forms

In the *Republic*, Plato (trans. 2006) presents his allegory of the cave. Let us envision a cave where shackled prisoners can only sit facing forward to observe shadows on a wall. One prisoner breaks free, turns around and sees that a fire is illuminating figures at an exit to the cave. The initial shock and pain of the light diminishes as the prisoner realizes that reality is beyond the shadows cast upon the cave wall. He climbs outside to see daylight. His eyes must again adjust, but initially he can see the reflection of objects in a pool of water. Eventually he is able to observe objects of the natural world bathed in sunlight. He returns to the cave to inform and rejoice with the others, but is instead met with disbelief and anger at his nonsensical talk of a "true" world.

The "shadows" represent the natural world of things, whereas the reflections in the pool can be regarded as analogous to our scientific and mathematical understanding of the world. The "true objects" in the analogy are Plato's notion of forms. This allegory serves as the basis for a metaphysics that influenced Aristotle, Christianity, and the development of science. As Pepper (1942) has explained, the philosophy of Plato and Aristotle derives from two root metaphors. The first is an artisan manufacturing an object (e.g., a horseshoe). The second employs an observation of nature whereby natural objects develop according to some internalized form or design (e.g., a rose, a dog). In each case there is a transcendent form that serves as the norm for the object in question. For Plato, these forms, as entities, are independent of the exemplars; in other words, forms exist even if they are never manifested in concrete reality. Differently for Aristotle, however, forms have no substance beyond their particulars in the material world, but are mere abstractions based on observations of the world.

Plato's distinction between an unchanging, idealistic world of forms and the flux of everyday life provides an explanation for how the Moirae operate in daily life. Our Moirae are imperfect reflections of our ultimate destiny that never perfectly manifest (an undesirable situation, as we would then lose our free will). Even individuals oriented toward greatness can deviate from their predestined paths. Our actual lives and personalities are not identical to the Platonic forms that influence us and draw us toward them. Our Moirae entice and inspire us toward our destinies but we are also trapped in Plato's cave where we can never fully realize our "ideal" selves, or our destiny.

Nietzsche's Eternal Recurrence

Nietzsche's often misunderstood and maligned philosophy is central to our discussion about destiny. Nietzsche is renowned for his philosophical concepts such as the "Ubermensch" and the "Will to Power," or the salacious details regarding his personal life. Pivotal to our investigation is his opposition to the Platonic philosophy discussed above and the development of his positive psychology. Nietzsche's intention was to undermine the destructive impact of Platonic philosophy on Western thought. Despite that much of his work railed against hyper-rationality and the abstraction of reality found in Western philosophy and religion, Nietzsche also developed psychological ideas which positively affirm the nature of life.

Arguably, the central concept in Nietzsche's teachings is that of "eternal return." Nietzsche contends that the physical structure of the universe is comprised of a never-ending, identically-recurring, circle of time compelling us to repeat our lives over and over, exactly as we have chosen. We are not certain whether Nietzsche intended this concept to be a nominal description of the universe; more importantly, he explored its psychological consequences as metaphors to live by: to positively affirm our lives such that we would want to relive every facet in precisely the same way again and again; to accept our basest acts and foibles as well as our achievements and qualities; to recognize that each thread in our human fabric is intricately woven together; to truly know that if we pull away a single strand from our life's fabric, it disintegrates with all of existence before us; to derive, not a sense of pessimism from this wisdom, but instead to shout "ONCE AGAIN!" from the nearest mountain top, ultimately endorsing life itself; to recognize that, by reinforcing our small but vital existence we also accept humanity.

Nietzsche's wish was that we seek an *Amor fati*. Indeed, one purpose of this book is to introduce the reader to the potential for loving one's own fate, but this is not to say that we resign ourselves to injustice, malice, and irresponsibility. Instead, we should celebrate our unique life circumstances as a central component of existence. Once we abandon our dismay of the past, we open ourselves to the reality of the future. Therefore, Nietzsche's philosophy represents one pillar of a fatalistic psychology.

Why is eternal recurrence the foundation of a fatalistic psychology? When we become capable through self-reflection and analysis to identify the behavioral patterns and psychological processes that dominate our lives, we can potentially grow into our true personhood. At that moment we may decide to make a clean break with the past and embark on a new direction, begin to use our talents, habits, and life patterns to move ourselves and others toward a compassionate acceptance of life.

Eternity: Recurrence and Forms

Next we will try to integrate these important and seemingly syncretic, philosophical concepts. The best way to appreciate how eternal recurrence, eternal forms, and the Moirae are fully manifested is to examine an actual life story, which we will do later in the chapter.

Eternity lies before us like a black hole that lures us, but it is not cyclical in the Nietzschean sense. Instead, it simply is. This naked eternity exists with our Moirae pulling us toward it. We will eventually meet our Moirae in the same way that celestial matter gravitates to black holes. The path we take may be slow or fast, direct or indirect. Either way, the gravitational pull of the Moirae is as strong as that of the black hole.

Furthermore, eternity has always existed and always will. It is outside time. The concept of time is only our subjective experience of the present and the past is just as vital as the present. The future meanwhile is unfolding before our clouded eyes. The decisions we make typically do not occur in discrete isolated acts, such as, Should I marry? What should my major be? What house should I buy? Shall I have children? Instead, our potential for free will is dispersed across a lifetime of activity, rarely evident in any single moment, but always there. It resembles what Sartre (1943/1983) has described as our "fundamental choice." Our free will is the melody of our lives, omnipresent, in every tune and it cannot be reduced to a singular note. Just as the meaning of a word is not derived from each letter, our "fundamental choice" has been made, is being made, and will be made throughout our lives, seldom at the conscious level. Our choices shape our destiny as much as our Moirae.

We therefore have a vision of destiny in which we are drawn to a Platonic form. Let us examine the life of Jesus in order to expand on this idea of eternity. In the next chapter we will grapple with the issue of how free will and destiny are intertwined.

Jesus: A Life of Destiny

Let us imagine that a social scientist is told that the person who will shape humanity over the next 2,000 years to the greatest extent is alive today. The task is to locate this person in a world of over six billion people. How might a sociologist or psychologist approach this dilemma? The social scientist would begin by identifying socioeconomic factors, cultural variables, economic ranking, family status, and personality disposition that would facilitate the greatest success and influence. Such linear reasoning would produce a pool of potential figures who are Westernized, born into elite backgrounds, well-educated, ambitious, from families wielding social and political power, emotionally stable, conscientious, extraverted, and exceedingly charismatic. We might allow our social scientist to narrow down the pool to 1,000 people. Would the Jesus figure be found? Perhaps. If the period happened to be that of ancient Greece, Socrates would have fit some of the criteria listed above.

However, if we examine the past 2,000 years, Jesus would undoubtedly have emerged as the most influential figure. But most would conclude that no social scientist, without the benefit of hindsight, could possibly have chosen this man as the most important figure in Western civilization, who would subsequently influence theologians as well as philosophers, scientists, and millions of people. For many individuals, Jesus represents the bedrock of their own reality. Why is it impossible to believe that a social scientist 2,000 years ago would necessarily choose someone like Jesus? This assumption rests on a fundamental flaw that potentially clouds our perception of human beings, a conceptualization that not only affects psychologists and their ilk, but also the media, novelists, politicians, and society: We have a "normalized" view of humanity (i.e., a view that emphasizes the average or typical) that excludes the possibility for greatness or destiny unless one belongs to a specific set of sociological and psychological categories. This "normalized" view of humanity is part of our Platonic legacy and the adaptation of statistical techniques within the social sciences. Personality variables such as extraversion and self-esteem exist as some idealized form to which we are mere shadows. The Moirae are also Platonic forms, but they call us to a future and neither dictate our past, present, nor our future behavior through an elusive genetic basis. We choose to say "yes" to the forms that invite us, or we can reject them. The decisions we make and the destiny we experience lays the foundation for our decision to proclaim "Yes" to it all again and again. Or we may choose to exist in a state of resentment toward the past, present, and future. Our free will lies not in choosing our destiny, character, or conditions but in a million, isolated, seemingly inconsequential behavioral decisions and in our fundamental emotional decision to fully accept every aspect of our lives.

How does the life of Jesus illustrate these conceptualizations of humanity? Jesus was born into a sociological and psychological nightmare with poor parents who did not have access to the same resources as many others in their time period. If we remove the significance of destiny from Jesus' life, his existence becomes a meaningless waste. However, many circumstances at the time of Jesus' conception and birth point to destiny. These events involve the parents of Jesus. An angel visits Joseph and announces, "She will bear a son and you are to name him Jesus, because he will save his people from their sins" (Matthew, 21). Later, Joseph is instructed how to protect his child and when to return to Israel. An angel informs Mary that she will give birth to a child despite her inexperience with the opposite sex. "He will be great and will be called son of the most high, and the Lord God will give him the throne of David his father, and he will rule over the house of Jacob forever, and of his kingdom there will be no end" (Luke, 32, 33). The angel continues, "The holy Spirit will come upon you, and the power of the Most High will overshadow you. Therefore the child to be born will be called holy, the Son of God" (Luke, 35); this is an immense calling for a poor, unmarried Galilean girl. After the birth, and somehow mysteriously aware of Jesus' destiny, Magi pay homage to the infant.

At this juncture, I may lose some of my scientific colleagues. Some might accuse me of espousing fundamentalist Christian principles under a pseudo-intellectual, post-modern guise. But nothing could be further from the truth. Fundamentalists of any religion make the same philosophical mistakes I have been lampooning here. The fundamentalist (and, in fact, most religious devotees) "essentialize" and "normalize" humanity, albeit different from academic psychologists and other social scientists. Instead, our aim is to illustrate how circumstances of fate, rather than assumptions about the past, enrich our understanding of humanity. However, it is now possible to argue that the Three Wise Men, Joseph's dreams, and Mary's vision are fairy tales without basis in reality. On this point, some of my readers and I may part ways; I would assert that stories about a person are intrinsic to the life narrative, regardless of their validity. It is irrelevant whether Mary's conversations with God were delusional or real, or whether these circumstances are embellishments of the Gospel writers. More important is that such tales probably helped Jesus to understand that he was destined for greatness, and that the stories about him profoundly influenced his disciples and later followers.

We know little about the early life of Jesus from scholarly or New Testament accounts. However, his teen years were likely filled with turbulence as he wrestled with the conflicting social and religious ideology emerging within him. At the age of twelve Jesus is lost by his parents for three days only to be found questioning the scholars in his "father's house" (Luke, 41-52).

As a young man Jesus embarks on his life of public destiny starting with an encounter with John the Baptist. Here it is announced, through a dramatic parting of the skies, that Jesus is the Son of God. Jesus is later tempted in the desert where he devotes his life to the calling that had earlier beckoned him. His commitment is clear and he begins his journey by attracting disciples. The magnitude of Jesus' destiny is less apparent during his ministry; however, his actions are repeatedly interpreted in terms of ancient prophecy by New Testament writers. Most important for our understanding of the Moirae are the final events in Jesus' life, beginning in the garden of Gethsemane where Jesus apparently develops a Zen-like acceptance of his impending fate. However, he continues to struggle with the betrayal and events he seems prescient of. He exerts enormous time and effort preparing psychologically and spiritually to fulfill his destiny. His free will and human qualities are captured in his appeal to God: "My Father, if it is possible, let this cup pass from me; yet, not as I will, but as you will" (Matthew, 39) and later in his prayer in the presence of scribes and elders, "My Father, if it is not possible that this cup pass without my drinking it, your will be done"! Jesus has the opportunity to defend himself and escape punishment. Yet he chooses not to. Again, with Pontius Pilate he has an opportunity to make a final appeal to an earthly authority. He refuses once again. The Gospels suggest that Jesus could easily have escaped being crucified by gaining the favor of the earthly authorities. He actively refuses the temptation and willfully affirms the path he has chosen. Total acceptance of his fate is revealed when he proclaims, "Father, forgive them, they know not what they do" (Luke, 34). That single heroic act of forgiveness indicates a complete *Amor Fati*. The reader is then aware that, indeed, Jesus would choose this path again and again with complete love for all humanity.

His human quality and the free will to doubt, however, are expressed in his last moments on the cross. Here we have an unusual situation of conflicting accounts among the Gospel writers; this is surprising, given their consistent interpretations at other critical junctures. According to Matthew (46) and Mark (34), Jesus cries out "My God, my God, why have you forsaken me?" Whereas, in the Gospel of Luke (46) he shouts, "Father, into your hands I commend my spirit." And, according to John (30), "It is finished." Perhaps Jesus stated all of these in his final hours on the cross; each utterance reveals his struggle with destiny.

The nature of Jesus' temptation is wonderfully illustrated in the novel *The Last Temptation of Christ*, by Nikos Kazantzakis (1960), and by a film of the same name by Scorsese and Ufland (1988). In the story Jesus is portrayed as being tempted by more than the lust, power, and greed of a desert devil. But these temptations are far more prosaic: a family life, sexual relations, children, and domestic tranquility. Although these portrayals are fictional interpretations, they are necessary to our discussion for two reasons. First, no one has privileged knowledge of the subjective, mental state of Jesus in his final hours. Therefore, Scorsese's screen portrayal is as reasonable and valid as any other. Second, the public reaction to the film was interesting. Fundamentalist Christians were outraged, allegedly by the scenes where Jesus imagines a different life which included marital relations. I, however, believe their anxiety stemmed from other concerns; that Jesus could have chosen a different life shakes the foundations of those who shun intellectual freedom and who seek absolute certainty. (This interpretation may also shed light on the conflicting Gospel accounts of Jesus on the cross.) However, the film was also widely acclaimed as a highly spiritual and inspiring portrait of Jesus. Jesus' final hours become particularly important in relation to our discussion of Nietzsche's idea of eternal recurrence and free will in his life.

Jesus, Platonic Forms, and Eternal Recurrence

As has been illustrated thus far, the life of Jesus was one of destiny. How then do the Moirae help us understand the nature of this destiny? Let us begin by acknowledging that Jesus' story, although unique, shares characteristics with other myths and religious stories. We can abstract from the details of Jesus' life, other lives and the narratives we tell, to inductively conclude that these stories share essential characteristics, a Platonic form, if you will. However, we need not engage in such intellectual labor, since the work has been completed for us by Joseph Campbell. Campbell was a religious scholar who built on the ideas of Jungian archetypes. (We discuss his work briefly in chapter seven.) According to Campbell (1949), the life story of Jesus fits the "hero archetype": a young man departs from his native land; he matures through immense difficulties, and has the opportunity to return as a redeemer. This scenario is found in religious stories and folktales. We therefore can observe the life of Jesus through the Platonic prism of the hero archetype. His life and interpretations of it were shaped by unconscious, narrative forms, which are our biological nature and cultural history. For Jesus, the hero archetype beckoned as a Moirae within the context of his personal, historical, and cultural context to shape his birth, life, and death.

But in other crucial ways Jesus was unlike any other person, even the "saviors" and heroes with whom he shares similarities. Most of us have had less access to, or are unfamiliar with, American Indian, African, Greek, and Asian folktales and the religious scripture cited by Campbell. Conversely, Jesus is an active, worldwide figure. One could argue that Jesus lived his destiny to the fullest. To take up such a discussion, however, would lead us astray from our central task, which is to explore the nature of the Moirae. Therefore, let us revisit how Nietzsche's concept of eternal recurrence and free will are manifest in the life of Jesus.

Nietzsche's positive psychology is built into various concepts including *Amor Fati*, eternal recurrence, his new morality, and the will to power. Throughout Jesus' life and in Nietzsche's work is the idea that God, morality, and greatness lie within us. It is a morality that celebrates life, yet accepts—and in Nietzsche's case celebrates—suffering. Jesus' life is filled with a sense of *Amor Fati*. Not only does the story of Jesus read like a cross between Campbell's hero myth and a Greek tragedy plot outline, but it is also representative of the pre-Socratic, Heraclitean idea that "character is fate." Reading the Gospels suggests that greatness was not only imposed upon Jesus, but that it was also an internal, unfolding plan determined by his heredity, personality, culture, historical situation, and ultimately, his free will. At times he struggles to accept the cup being passed to him, but he does accept it without resentment and even forgives the perpetrators. What a love of life!

Nietzsche (1882/1982) poses the following dilemma in *The Gay Science* to illustrate his concept of eternal recurrence:

How, if some day or night a demon were to sneak after you into your loneliest loneliness and say to you, This life as you now live it and have lived it, you will have to live once more and innumerable times more; and there will be nothing new in it, but every pain and every joy and every thought and sigh and every-thing immeasurably small or great in your life must return to you—all in the same succession and sequence—even this spider and this moonlight between the trees, and even this moment and I myself. 'The eternal hourglass of exis-tence is turned over and over, and you with it, a dust grain of dust.' Would you not throw yourself down and gnash your teeth and curse the demon who spoke thus? Or did you once experience a tremendous moment when you would have answered him, 'You are a god, and never have I heard anything more godly.' If this thought were to gain possession of you, it would change you, as you are, or perhaps crush you. The question in each and every thing, 'Do you desire this once more and innumerable times more?' would weigh upon your actions as the greatest stress. Or how well disposed would you have to become to yourself and to life to crave nothing more fervently than this ultimate eternal confirma-tion and seal? (pp. 101–02).

It is difficult to believe that Jesus would not have accepted the entirety of his life; it is also difficult to imagine his resentment, regret, and remorse over the choices he made. Envisage Jesus gnashing his teeth and cursing the demon who spoke to him. Instead, his life was filled with courage, responsibility, joy, and acceptance. He spent each moment becoming who he was in the affirmation of this earthly life.

Jesus also exemplifies a will to power. Throughout his life he rejects ordi-nary hedonism and ancient Jewish teachings in the service of a new morality. His path seems to have been forged by a spiritual, unconsciousness beyond the scope of his understanding, and at times outside of his own awareness. Jesus' choices evoke the images of self-sacrifice in service to a greater virtue and mo-rality. His life represents a journey of self-mastery in following his ultimate des-tiny on the cross, and reflects his desire to fundamentally change the world and express his nature as the will to power.

Conclusion

Let us close this chapter by summarizing how our discussion of Nietzsche's eternal recurrence, Plato's ideal forms, and the life of Jesus illustrate the tenets of an unconscious fatalism. We first note that the ideal form of the Moirae and the question posed by Nietzsche's demon regarding eternal recurrence exists predominantly at the unconscious level, in part as a collective, unconscious phe-nomenon at the human level, but also within the individual unconscious. There-fore, the hero "archetype" is part of our biological, collective unconscious that shapes how we construct narratives and how we live. However, for Jesus this biological, shared unconscious unfolds in a unique way. At the individual level he becomes and is the son of God. The Moirae biologically provided Jesus with unconscious access not only to a shared archetype, but also to a destiny of one-ness with the ultimate ideal form of God. Two important implications about this statement should be clarified. First, Jesus was granted a unique opportunity that

we will never face. Although we are provided through our collective unconscious archetypes and ideal forms of the "hero myth" and God, we are not called
to become God. Tomorrow, I could decide that I am the son of God. It would
not happen, despite the fact of my free will. Considering my history, culture,
biology, and psychology, such a pronouncement would likely result in my being
prescribed with a pharmaceutical. Second, and more controversial, Jesus accepted his fate. It is conceivable to think that others were at that time "called by
God" but did not respond, or at some point chose not to fulfill their destiny. To
some, this may sound like heresy, but I believe it is consistent with much of the
Christian tradition; that is, that the laypersons' Christian view of life can be
summarized as: God provides us with gifts, choices, and opportunities along the
path of life and we are free to choose or not. Why would this not be the case
with Jesus? Was he not human? His Moirae undoubtedly seized him and shook
him to his core, but at the same time he forgave his persecutors and, on repeat
occasions, chose not to escape his destiny.

Jesus remains with us today because of the cyclical nature of the Moirae.
His story is replayed through such ritualistic celebrations as the Catholic mass,
communion, Easter celebrations, and the liturgical year. The entire year of a
devoted Christian therefore entails the reenactment of the life of Jesus through
ritual and celebration. The "ONCE AGAIN!" that Jesus shouted during his
earthly lifetime, in response to every moment of his life, has resulted in the eternal recurrence of his life through ritual and devotion. This affirms not only his
selfhood but also all of humanity and life itself.

Part Three: Free Will

Chapter 5

My Genes Made Me do it, Unconsciously! Free Will, Fatalism, and Morality

"Freedom and determinism give birth to each other. Every advance in freedom gives birth to a new determinism, and every advance in determinism gives birth to a new freedom. Freedom is a circle within a larger circle of determinism, which is, in turn, surrounded by a larger circle of freedom. And so on ad infinitum." –Rollo May (1981, p. 84)

"If you please to plant yourself on the side of Fate, and say, Fate is all; then we say, a part of fate is the freedom of man."
–Ralph Waldo Emerson (1860/1981, p. 358)

"Man is condemned to be free."
–Jean-Paul Sartre (1957/2004, p. 350)

We often observe the daily struggle of individuals trying to change their lives. However, there are a number of common culturally-defined periods when we attempt a regime of self-improvement; New Year's resolutions, milestone birthdays, entrance to college, divorce, and the loss of a loved one all spring to mind as potential spurs to self-transformation. However, the statistics on ability to change are startling in terms of failure rates. Polivy and Herman (2002) reviewed the evidence for health-related behaviors and reported that studies indicate that an overwhelming majority of smokers, gamblers, alcoholics, and dieters fail, and continue to fail to change behaviors. For example, 25% of New Year's resolutions are abandoned by the start of the second week (Norcross, Ratzin, & Payne, 1989). One well-known New Year's resolution is to lose weight. However, 95% of dieters regain the lost weight within a few years (Heatherton, Mahamedi, Striepe, Field, & Keel, 1997). Moreover, the impact of sporadic dieting on the body is well publicized in the media. Another common New Year's resolution is to quit smoking. An estimated 75 to 80% of smokers who quit were unable to resist smoking for one year (Prochaska, Velicer, Guadagnoli, Rossi, & DiClemente, 1991). Other attempts at self-improvement, for example, a concerted attitude towards academic study, have similar failure rates (Polivy & Herman, 1999).

Dangerously addictive behaviors are even more tenacious. As the most frequently studied addiction, alcohol abuse research has indicated consistently high rates of relapse. Allsop and Saunders (1989) report that 45-50% of alcoholics in treatment programs resume their normal level of alcohol consumption within one year, and 90% have returned to some level of alcohol consumption within three months. Similar failure rates are found for gamblers, with Brown (1989) reporting a 93% relapse rate after two years for individuals in Gamblers Anonymous. To make matters worse, the Polivy and Herman review (2002) shows that research conducted over the past few decades indicates consistent rates of failure to change.

Despite dismal statistics and personal experience, we nevertheless maintain an overwhelming insistence that personal transformation and change is possible. Given these statistics and the theoretical model that I have delineated in this book, we must ask ourselves if there is any role for free will in the human experience. We address this primary concern by examining how this issue has been addressed by psychologists. We will then analyze the implications of the Moirae relative to how we think about and respond to human behavior by specifically examining the role of forgiveness and redemption.

Psychoanalysis, Existentialism, and Determinism

Psychoanalytic thinkers and existentialists have traditionally been the most willing to grapple with the issues of free will and determinism during the past century. They have delved into their complexity, and their findings are central to a deeper understanding of the Moirae.

On the one hand, there is a strong determinist element in psychoanalytic theory beginning with Freud's postulation that our unconscious and early childhood experiences, which are beyond our current awareness, inevitably dictate our present behavior. On the other hand, psychoanalytic theory is wedded to psychoanalytic practice, which asserts some human capacity for change. There are, moreover, clear divergences within psychoanalysis on the role of free will. The divergence of opinion can best be highlighted by our survey of the ideas of Freud along with existential thinkers and psychoanalysts, such as Jean-Paul Sartre and Rollo May, who stand on opposite sides of the spectrum.

Sigmund Freud created a deeply deterministic, albeit utterly innovative, theory of human identity and behavior during a profoundly transformative place and time in history: 19th century Europe. Freud's theory attributes unconscious conflicts and psychic energy to the formation of adult behavior. Freud has designated that the personality structure comprises the id, the ego, and the superego but the id, which is unconscious and instinctual, predominates. The id is primarily composed of sexual and aggressive impulses that operate according to the *pleasure principle*. These impulses are supposedly irrational and remain our primary energy source for the personality throughout life: it manifests in dreams, fantasies, and aberrational behaviors. Our adult personality, however, over time becomes more ego-centered and abides by the *reality principle*. This developmental evolution happens in accordance with psychosexual stages. Freud also asserted that childhood personality development corresponds to *erogenous zones* where libidinal impulses are satisfied, depending upon an individual's age. For example, during the first two years of life we embody the oral stage where libidinal tensions are alleviated through oral satisfaction. The result of this development is a mechanistic personality structure driven by psychic energies that must be satisfied and that operate according to psychological rules delineated by Freud. He employed these general, theoretical concepts to explain his patients' behavior, and regarded these deterministic processes as irrational as well as outside of our awareness. The only way to rein them in was through psychoanalysis, which would cultivate the patient's ability to rationally control or redirect the unconscious drives. Freud seems to suggest that we can exercise a modicum of free will through rational thinking, but he never fully analyzed the relationship between free will and determinism. Freud regarded himself as a scientist able to discern structures, processes, and laws of human behavior and consciousness. Although most of his concepts cannot be proved empirically, he did seek general laws in order to explain individual cases, which is the hallmark of the scientific process. This aim differentiates him from the existentialists.

A discussion of existentialism and psychology is likely to begin with Martin Heidegger's philosophy and the movement known as *phenomenology*. Psychologists who have employed phenomenological principles in the pursuit of human psychological insights include Medard Boss and Ludwig Binswanger. Indeed, both men reject determinism and thus have an important and unique place in the field of psychology. However, these existential psychologists did not explore the relationship between free will and determinism, and instead were mostly interested in developing phenomenology as an alternative technique to the scientific method. Therefore, we will focus on existential psychologists who have intentionally wrestled with the philosophical aspects of free will and determinism.

Although known primarily as a philosopher, Jean-Paul Sartre's philosophy has tremendous implications for psychological theorizing in general, and is directly related to our discussion, in particular regarding the role of free will with a fatalistic theory like the Moirae. We therefore begin by understanding Sartre's existential psycho-theorizing and especially its relationship to Freud's classic psychoanalysis.

In *Being and Nothingness* Sartre (1943/1983) sets out his theory of consciousness and illustrates its differences with psychoanalytic theory. Sartre vehemently objects to Freud's emphasis on determination in psychoanalysis. He also rejects the principle of determinism featured in Freud's use of general principles to understand individual psychology. Sartre's critique is not limited to Freud but includes all psychoanalysts who would generally apply the scientific method to human behavior. His criticism therefore extends beyond Freud to contemporary scientific psychology, which remains today deterministic and reliant on general principles in order to explain individual behavior.

As we have seen, Freud sought a comprehensive theory in order to explain individual dynamics by using general, psychoanalytic principles. Freud emphasized the unconscious and particularly childhood development, which operates according to universal principles which then dictate adult functioning. Sartre, however, sees the person's "fundamental project" as central to one's own understanding of behavior. Sartre (1943/1983) describes, "Thus the best way to conceive of the fundamental project of human reality is to say that man is the being whose project is to be God. . . . To be man means to reach toward being God. Or if you prefer, man fundamentally is the desire to be God" (p. 724). McAdams (1994) clarifies, "The lifelong process of creating the self is what Sartre called the fundamental project. Through the fundamental project, the person continually questions who he or she is and searches for more authentic ways of being in the world" (p. 426). The fundamental project is the transcendent meaning of an individual's actions. Sartre employed this concept to understand the meaning of a human life. For example, he sought to understand the fundamental project the French writer Gustav Flaubert (Sartre, 1981) and others through psychobiography which emphasized the creation of meaning through personal myths. Sartre's approach is a radical departure from the psychobiography with a psychoanalytic perspective. For example, in Freud's (1910/1984) *Leonardo da Vinci: A Memory of his Childhood*, he examined Leonardo's supposed unresolved libidinal conflicts in order to explain his art and life.

Sartre's fundamental project resembles the Moirae in some respects, but my theory presents contingencies in life as emergent from one's *future* unconscious, one's personal Moirae, that is, individual fate or destiny. Sartre's fundamental project is a freely chosen product of one's consciousness. In his early writings Sartre provides little in-depth examination of life's contingencies and instead emphasizes the power of human freedom. He acknowledges that some forces are beyond one's control, but he nevertheless focuses on the free will we have in those situations. For example, there is a famous passage in *Being and Nothingness* where Sartre discusses a prisoner in chains who remains free because of his ability to interpret and give meaning to his situation.

Sartre's explanation for behavior avoids the typical scientific approach of seeking general principles to explain individual behavior. For example, trait psychologists may employ the term extraversion to explain friendly, gregarious behavior. When asked about the origin of extraversion, many will point to biological variables, increasingly genetic predispositions, and infant temperament, which can lead to the question: why do certain gene patterns result in extraversion? Trait psychologists declare that that question is outside the realm of psychology and thus are unable to provide us with a satisfactory answer. For Sartre, the fundamental project does not operate as a causal theoretical principle but rather, is interpretative. The individual experiences which comprise a person's life give rise to a fundamental project. The fundamental project provides meaning, not causal explanation, for the individual life. The Moirae is more serious in accepting the fact that human contingencies are real factors for determining behavior. However, Sartre's emphasis on free will is important for two reasons; he places the roots of human free will within consciousness, and he acknowledges that humans always have the capacity to exhibit free will, even when interpreting one's existence in a prison cell. These points are consistent with the Moirae in that they acknowledge that human free will arises from consciousness, past determinants are not the primary cause of present behavior, and general scientific principles cannot effectively explain individual behavior. The Moirae recognizes that each person's biological, psychological, and social structure draws them into particular life paths.

As mentioned previously, a variety of psychologists have applied existential principles to psychology, including Binswanger and Frankl. But perhaps the most thorough examiner of the role of free will and fatalism in a psychological framework has been Rollo May. In *Freedom and Destiny* (1981) his definition of destiny is that, "Destiny is a cognate of the term *destination*, which implies moving toward a goal. . . . I define *destiny* as the pattern of limits and talents that constitutes the 'givens' in life" (italics in original, p. 89). Furthermore, he illustrates how destiny operates on a number of levels. For example, May indicates that destiny may operate on a "cosmic" level where birth and death phenomena operate and we exhibit little control. There are also "genetic" and "cultural" levels where our gender and other physical characteristics are provided and the familial, social, and historical contingencies of our existence operate, respectively. Finally, he discusses the "circumstantial," which are perhaps chance historical happenings, as in war. May also indicates that we have various ways to approach the destiny we face—moving from a relatively passive, stoic stance—to increasing levels of engagement. The levels include "cooperation," "awareness and acknowledgment," "engagement," "confronting and challenging," and "encountering and rebelling."

I agree with Rollo May on the role of fate. And while we share some views, there are important differences between his conception of destiny and the Moirae. Most importantly, May describes destiny in terms of our past or present manifest in our genes, family, culture, and so on; whereas I conceptualize destiny as a preexisting archetypal, unconscious process to which we are drawn across our lifespan. Although May tries to distinguish between determinism and destiny, his distinction is one of nomenclature and subject only. May claims that humans possess consciousness and are therefore not *determined* in the sense that other animals or objects may be. However, this distinction is a problematic feature of his idea. The theory of the Moirae maintains the important role of consciousness in giving birth to free will. However, consciousness ultimately rests on biology which is causally determined. Furthermore, consciousness (and therefore free will) develops along an evolutionary continuum contingent on biological development and functioning. I therefore suggest that free will is expanding with the evolutionary development of consciousness. Such an idea implies that some non-human animals could have a degree of capacity for free will, and that human beings have varying capacities for it. Capacity differs between individual people and within each person's lifetime. For example, surely our capacity for free will is decreased as infants, or if we were to enter into a coma.

Our discussion thus far regarding the Moirae has taken a sharply deterministic turn; however, this is not the time to undermine the role of free will as espoused by existential philosophers and psychologists, but rather the contrary; unlike Freud's unconscious, the future unconscious within the Moirae framework is not exclusively deterministic. It does not constrain us necessarily in the choices that we make. It is a future unconscious which has well worn paths and easy choices. It is a fate which leads us but does not dictate. We may choose not to traverse the well worn path or we may instead choose to trudge through the underbrush, and push aside the thorny branches where no clear path lies. We may find ourselves on a mountain peak, or even on an avalanche. We do not know. Furthermore, staying on a pre-destined path, although not romantic, may be the best choice for us. The point is that there is a role for free will and self-determination. The personal, future, archetypal unconscious does not dictate our present choices. Instead, it clears paths for us. It presents opportunities for us. It can even nudge us in particular directions, but ultimately, the choices are ours.

We are no more constrained by our personal unconscious than we are by our environments, past conflicts in the unconscious, or stimulus-response patterns. We are not merely driven and propelled by the past. Similarly, the future provides us with the free will to choose well-worn paths or potentially dangerous, untrodden land. As Emerson (1860/1981) observed, "A man's power is hooped in by a necessity which by many experiments, he touches on every side until he learns its arc" (p. 356). In other words, we make choices within contexts; choices which will make life easy for us, choices which will make life difficult, choices which are morally responsible, and/or choices which are morally irresponsible. An easy choice for one person may be the morally responsible choice for another and vice versa. We need therefore to consider each choice in light of each person's Moirae.

What then can be the role of the psychologist? As this discussion also sheds light on the moral evaluation of others we must realize that for some individuals the personal, future unconscious which possesses them makes it either easy or difficult to make correct moral choices. However, for others these same choices are nearly impossible to make. For some it may be all too easy to make morally irresponsible choices. Once again, I should reiterate that ultimately this fact does not negate personal responsibility. Instead, individuals need to become aware of their personal unconscious and recognize the patterns which occur within the future unconscious, cyclical behaviors, and the cognitions which seize them. They are sometimes morally obligated to choose a less worn path. An awareness of the future unconscious is as important, and I would argue *more* important, than the resolution of past unconscious conflicts. Freud understood the difficulty in amending the past and resolving past conflicts. The future, however, is not yet written and future choices are less determined. And although future paths are once again clear and easy to follow, they have not yet been traversed by us. Although we are driven by destiny, we are nevertheless responsible for our actions.

Free will, as it pertains to our discussion of the Moirae, is often taken for granted as an easily obtained commodity, but for our purposes, that idea is anathema. In fact, free will is a rather limited product of human consciousness; it is most easily exercised in the development and formation of attitudes and preferences. However, even in these instances the exhibition of free will is a struggle. And, for an individual to develop a new behavior or a goal-oriented pattern of behaviors that *deviate* from his or her Moirae, is indeed a Herculean task. Free will is, I suggest, not the norm but the likely exception. We must take care in this discussion not to assume that a free act is necessarily a culturally qualified "moral" act. It is of course possible to exhibit free will in the service of either good or evil. It is normal for us to presume that such widely admired figures as Martin Luther King, Jr., Mahatma Gandhi, or Mother Teresa faced moral choices and made courageous decisions to choose the difficult moral and spiritual high road. However, let us consider that their individual Moirae may have allowed for these decisions to be easier for them than some other path. A similar notion is often borne out in the sentiments of figures who claim that they had little or no choice in critical situations. Nevertheless, the moral correctness of their actions and their higher spiritual development remains accessible in historical accounts. We can, however, scrutinize the role of choice in their actions. Let us consider that *it may be* that the anonymous, blue-collar laborer living alone down the street has successfully battled overwhelming homicidal urges his entire life and has exhibited more free will than our typical moral exemplars. It seems that we may have confused the issue of exemplary behavior and freedom. The Greeks admired their heroes but also saw their lot as one of destiny, not of personal choice. Examples of this are best found in the epic poetry of the Greeks where the heroes affirm the noblest of values while clearly being at the whim of larger forces (Hatab, 1990).

The existentialists asserted that meaning and moral choice were inherently linked to freedom. However, many existentialist writers eventually acknowledged the important role that deterministic elements play in life. Sartre moved from an extreme position trumpeting free will in *Being and Nothingness* to later emphasizing the contingencies of human experience and the powerful role of the social order.

Psychologists who had adopted an existential approach were also forced to ultimately deal with the limited role of free will. This is best exhibited in Rollo May's (1981) *Freedom and Destiny* whereby he delineates the role of destiny in human behavior. Many of his ideas about destiny are similar to those developed in this book. Although May acknowledges the impact of destiny, he ascribes more free will to humans than that which is conceptualized through the Moirae.

Being aware of our Moirae and our destiny paradoxically gives rise to freedom. May makes a similar point when he states that freedom and determinism give birth to each other. He cites two interesting examples. Freud's discovery of unconscious childhood conflicts, which cause us to react irrationally, seems to take away our free will. However, this deterministic theorizing actually has the potential to loosen us from those very deterministic forces through therapy and self-awareness. Secondly, Darwin's theory of evolution showed how we are the products of the deterministic forces of natural selection. Once again, this knowledge not only frees us to understand our ancestral past, but also to employ evolutionary principles in a purposeful way.

How can we apply knowledge of the Moirae to our everyday lives? Let us return to the examples of resolutions and opportunities for change. By being aware of limitations and constraints, we can approach change and employ our free will in potentially fruitful ways. Being aware of our Moirae as manifested in life-patterns of addictions or maladaptive behaviors compels us to recognize that personal transformation is not simply a matter of personal resolve and commitment, but one of identifying consistencies and parameters in our characters, and acknowledging that radical transformations are sometimes necessary in order to change our lives for the better.

We have learned that our behaviors are shaped predominantly by a *future unconscious* that pulls us in certain directions and life paths on the basis of our particular Moirae. As a result, we have a limited capacity for free will. This is especially true in a case where the Moirae seize control of us (e.g., serious illness). The question now arises, what are the practical applications of the principles discussed above? In other words, how do we discern between behaviors based on the Moirae versus our own free will? The simple answer is that it is extremely difficult to discern the difference between truly free actions and those predominantly influenced by our Moirae. But there are clues. For example, if someone is engaged in cyclically-oriented behaviors as discussed in chapter three, the continuance of those behaviors is almost surely an example of the Moirae in action. However, if someone is able to transcend those circular behaviors, has he or she then exhibited free will? Not necessarily. The person who has abused alcohol in a cyclical manner *for years or even decades* may be finally exerting his or her free will to break from the chain of dependency. It *may* be that a genetically-based phenomenon has altered that person's biology so that he or she responds differently to alcohol. A shift in biological functioning may influence personal resolve, cognitions regarding alcohol, and the specific physiological response to alcohol that differs from past years. An altered physiology means that the person could be genetically determined to stop using at a particular age period in the same way that someone who is allergic to alcohol never really has the opportunity to abuse alcohol. Or, it may be that the altered physiology now allows the person to exhibit some degree of free will. Finally, it is possible that putting away the bottle is an act of sheer free will. It is impossible to tell.

A discussion of causality can be further complicated if we ask recovering alcoholics whether free will played a role in their decision; many are likely to answer "Yes"! We should distinguish between the phenomenological *feeling* of free will and *actual* free will, but we cannot. The waters become even muddier when we discuss future behavior. How do I know that the choice I am about to make is freely determined, or whether it is the product of my Moirae? Is the life path I am embarking on now dictated by my *future personal unconscious* calling me to my destiny? Is my intuition the product of my Moirae or of my free will?

In order to prevent confusion it may be fruitful to advise an "as if" strategy for resolving these personal dilemmas; that is, we should almost always act "as if" free will exists and that we are exerting it, except in cases where we clearly see the hand of the Moirae. When we act "as if" free will exists, then human consciousness is like an egg waiting to hatch its own possibilities: for some people the Moirae will dictate their destinies; for others free will is successfully exerted and the general principles of science rooted in the biology of the Moirae can be transcended. Consistent with the "as if" idea is the Greek attitude toward limitations of life. Hatab (1990) indicates that Greek religion treated limitations with "divine laughter" (p. 54). He adds, ". . . laughter stems from the recognition of a limit and is therefore in a way linked to the tragic. Humanity, though kin to the gods, is separated from them by mortality and the degree of powerlessness. . . . We can see, then, how the idea of limitation, the central element of Greek religion, could generate the two luminous art forms, comedy and tragedy, for which the Greeks deserve our everlasting gratitude" (p. 54). Furthermore, even though the Greeks recognized the role of fate, they still emphasized "the heroic pursuit of excellence" (p. 53). Nietzsche's celebration of "Dionysian wisdom" is also similar; Nietzsche accepts the suffering and destruction of life because they are intricately linked to the human capacity for creation, which he extols as our highest value (Reginster, 2006).

Let us now compare these interrelated ideas regarding the nature of human freedom to Sartre's ideas of free will in order to better illustrate the nature of the Moirae. Sartre provides an analysis of human freedom with an example of a gambler who returns to the gaming table after once again having resolved to quit. The example is lengthy but worth quoting verbatim from *Being and Nothingness* (pp. 69–71).

> It is that of the gambler who has freely and sincerely decided not to gamble anymore and who, when he approaches the gaming table, suddenly sees all his resolutions melt away. This phenomenon has often been described as if the sight of the gaming table reawakened in us a tendency which entered into conflict with our former resolution and ended by drawing us in spite of this. Aside from the fact that such a description is done in materialistic terms and peoples the mind with opposing forces (there is, for example, the moralists' famous 'struggle of reason with the passions'), it does not account for the facts. In reality—the letters of Dostoevsky bear witness to this—there is nothing in us which resembles an inner *debate* as if we had to weigh motives and incentives before deciding. The earlier resolution of 'not playing anymore' is always *there*, and in the majority of cases the gambler when in the presence of the gaming table, turns toward it as if to ask it for help; for he does not wish to play, or rather having taken his resolution the day before, he thinks of himself still as not wishing to play anymore; he believes in the effectiveness of this resolution. But what he apprehends then in anguish is the total inefficacy of the past resolution. It is there doubtless but fixed, ineffectual, surpassed by the very fact that I am conscious *of* it. The resolution is still *me* to the extent that I realize constantly my identity with myself across the temporal flux, but it is no

longer me—due to the fact that it has become an object *for* my consciousness. I am not subject to it, it fails in the mission, which I have given it. The resolution is there still, I *am* it in the mode of not-being. What the gambler apprehends at this instant is again the permanent rupture in determinism. . . . I perceive with anguish that *nothing* prevents me from gambling. The anguish *is me* since by the very fact of taking my position in existence as consciousness of being, I make myself *not to be* the past of good resolution *which I am*. It would be in vain to object that the sole condition of this anguish is ignorance of the underlying psychological determinism. . . . This freedom which reveals itself to us in anguish can be characterized by the existence of that *nothing* which insinuates itself between motives and act. It is not *because* I am free that my act is not subject to the determination of motives; on the contrary, the structure of motives as ineffective is the condition of my freedom (italics in original).

Sartre suggests that there are no motives within consciousness that determine our gambling behavior. In this moment of anguish where he says *nothing* is stopping us from gambling, we are experiencing free will. Indeed, for anyone the moment of temptation is filled with anguish and we do experience the potential for the freedom to choose an alternative act. Here is a fundamental difference between Sartre's examination of freedom and that posited within the Moirae. The phenomenological experience of a motivation toward something should not be assumed to be a causal force, as Sartre asserts. However, the biology behind the experience of a motivation is a causal force. The gambler faced with the anguish of temptation is not experiencing free will, as Sartre asserts. Instead, I would argue, that the gambler is experiencing the opposite; that is the biology or limitations of his existence. His biology is rooted in neural reward circuits molded by his experiences and genetic composition. Indeed, the *opportunity* for freedom lies in the moment of the gambler's anguish but it is not his actual free will. It is his lack of freedom that causes his anguish. It is an anguish whereby someone, with a different personal future unconscious, would not at all experience as anguish.

Forgiveness & Redemption

We have learned that, on a personal basis, we may typically want to act "as if" free will always exists while acknowledging that this is not always true. However, there are three instances where it may be best to instead openly admit to the powerful role of everyone's future personal unconscious. First, when examining our past, we can as previously mentioned, search for patterns that reveal our personal Moirae. Second, we can probe for similar patterns in those with whom we have close personal relationships. We will recognize other's Moirae operative not only in their lives but also in how the Moirae interact (a topic worthy of investigation would be to explore how the Moirae/fates operate on the interpersonal level, supporting, attracting, and repelling each other between individuals). Finally, we see how the Moirae underpin societal problems. In each of these cases, understanding the power of the Moirae can lead us to a morality emphasizing forgiveness and redemption rather than punishment and retribution.

Acknowledging the powerful role that the Moirae plays in all life can indeed help us develop a sense of understanding, tolerance, and forgiveness in regard to human behavior. This same knowledge can simultaneously lead us to free will and change. Because, although we acknowledge that behavior is often the function of fatalism complexly expressed through each individual's future unconsciousness via a circumscribed biology, culture, and set of family conditions, this perception of human limitation also allows for self-reflection—and leads not to guilt or self-justification—but instead to honest self-appraisal. For example, the drug/alcohol addict may need to permanently and completely withdraw from any opportunity for abusing, or else begin to profoundly alter their own biology and social environment. The obese individual may require radical surgery to change his or her biology, or may otherwise have to accept themselves as they are, along with the ramifications associated with self-acceptance.

Seeking harmful patterns in our past behavior is a difficult endeavor requiring integrity and self-analysis; it is moreover, a difficult process to perform accurately prior to mid-life. During the teen years and through the twenties, behavior may directly be the result of our immediate circumstances. Usually only after time has separated us from events do we begin to see patterns emerge across our life-span. However, patterns can be observed at any age. Parents in particular have identified distinct early behavioral patterns in their children that have carried on through their lives.

The relative ease of being able to identify early behaviors is noteworthy; perhaps it is easier to see life patterns exhibited by others, especially our loved ones and close friends. We know what tempts them and what activities they are drawn towards, often better than they do themselves. We can identify how our patterns interrelate with siblings, parents, spouses, and children. Indeed, the knowledge of each other's Moirae within close relationships may help to explain why there can be greater levels of acceptance and forgiveness than in other everyday relationships. Loving others may include knowing and accepting their Moirae. Children, parents, and siblings are linked to us not only through similar environments and experiences but also, generally, through similar biological and genetic backgrounds. Talents and abilities, whether they are musical, athletic, or academic, often permeate entire extended families.

We now come to the issue of how knowledge of the Moirae can influence how we approach recurrent social problems. Since we have discussed addictive behaviors throughout these chapters, let us next explore how our knowledge of a personal, future unconscious may influence social policy. The research literature on addiction indicates that abstinence-only themed programs (e.g., Alcoholics Anonymous), which stress total cessation of drug use, have not shown high success rates (for reviews see Pinel, 2006; Sue, Sue, & Sue, 2000). Given our now deeper understanding of the Moirae, it is clear why such programs are often ineffective. Overwhelming biological, cultural, and social factors are not simply overcome through the completion of a 12-step program. However, other approaches that emphasize harm-reduction strategies, multi-modal approaches, and phased withdrawal (e.g., methadone treatment), and/or the radical restructuring of the addicted person's life through therapeutic communities have better overall rates of success for many individuals (for reviews see Maisto, Galizio, & Connors, 1991; Ksir, Hart, & Ray, 2006; Sue, Sue, & Sue, 2000). Societies that emphasize decriminalization and management of issues surrounding drug abuse (e.g., crime) also have had better success rates (see Pinel, 2006). In both cases, we find reduced rates of criminal activity and higher rates of employment, thus benefiting the individual and society. If we consider the large percentage of federal and state inmates incarcerated for drug offenses, we can easily imagine the heavy burden imposed upon the criminal justice system; whereas the implementation of health-based, harm-reduction control systems seems more appropriate, given the power of the Moirae and the availability of drugs and alcohol in contemporary societies.

Finally, violence, aggression, and the criminal justice system embody another noteworthy problem in the United States. Our discussion of the Moirae indicates that free will is a rare product of consciousness, and that we are subservient to the dictates of our personal, future unconscious. Therefore, we suspect that the violent criminal usually comes from a dysfunctional household, has a lower socio-economic status, may be genetically predisposed toward violence, has little education, and actively seeks to view and/or has been unwittingly overexposed to media violence. All of these factors have been thrust upon the individual with no real choice. This person's Moirae have called him toward a life of violence at a very early age. Most individuals born into dangerous environments respond accordingly with violent behavior as a means of coping, as well as an inability to behave differently. How then do we treat this person?

I suggest too that neither the traditional conservative nor the liberal ideas are consistent with the Moirae. For example, not only is the "rehabilitation" approach inconsistent with many of the ideas in the Moirae but it is also inconsistent with research on the effectiveness of rehabilitation programs. On the other hand, the notion that each person consciously "chooses" their behaviors, and therefore all violent criminals should be incarcerated and punished, is also inconsistent with the Moirae. What advice might we offer society in light of the theoretical ideas put forward here? First, there is a clear subgroup of the population that is violent and dangerous to society and has little likelihood for "rehabilitation." Therefore, this group needs to be separated from society. This is already accomplished through our penal system. There is no need for punitive reactions. However, I would argue in favor of education and therapy to increase self-awareness of life patterns. If we remove the retribution element from the arena, then there may also be the opportunity to rejoin society. Furthermore, it is obvious that most violence occurs among young males who also have substance abuse problems. With time, the age and abuse problems could be addressed with the possibility that violent offenders may partially rejoin society in mid-life through lengthy paroles and/or half-way communities. We should also give credence to whether or not there is a clear and consistent pattern of violence, which should be considered when determining guilt or innocence and the appropriate sentence. Rehabilitation should focus on job training that moves prisoners immediately out of prison to jobs with continual monitoring until old-age. In other words, it may be possible to reduce the numbers of those incarcerated but to nevertheless monitor individuals exhibiting aggressive behavior. The problems of addiction and violence—especially—call for practical and immediate measures.

Our discussion thus far regarding personal responsibility, individual behavior, and social implications in families and social policies, compels us to revisit the issues raised above. On the one hand, most of us would acknowledge the influence of what existentialists have called "throwness," which is our individually inherited social and historical situations; other factors such as race, family, and culture are also components of the Moirae. On the other hand, we also expect that we are able to transcend this "throwness" and exert our free will. However, as our discussion of the Moirae has made apparent, this is far more difficult than we may have previously assumed. If we accept the limitation that free will is difficult to exert, individuals can indeed become despondent or even think life to be meaningless. However, this is where the existentialists and other contemporary postmodern writers can help lead us out of this maze of despair. Keep in mind that, although the existentialists acknowledge all the contingencies into which we are born, they also believe that, ultimately, we have the possibility and even the duty to create our lives. How might we approach this endeavor? In the previous section, I recommended that we should adopt an "as if" approach to free will, and that we should approach our lives with a sense of free will while cognitively acknowledging that this is not always true. Our dilemma is similar to that faced by many postmodernists, who confronted the pit of nihilism after deconstructing all meaning in the world. Gergen (1991) argues that we should consider the world as a "serious game," where we approach life in earnest, but meanwhile accepting that *meaning* is historically and culturally-bound. Furthermore, he draws parallels with our approach to sporting events where we "give it our all" on the field, but afterwards acknowledge that "it's just a game." Adopting an "as if" approach provides us with opportunities to express our free will and also to create meaningful life stories during times of struggle—when the Moirae are in control and free will is out of reach.

Part Four: Unifying Contemporary Psychology with The Moirae

Chapter 6

What Would Freud and Darwin Think? Psychoanalysis and Evolutionary Psychology

"We are a psychic process which we do not control, or only partly direct. Consequently, we cannot have any final judgment about ourselves or our lives."
– C. G. Jung (1989, p. 4)

"From the beginning I had a sense of destiny, as though my life was assigned to me by fate and had to be fulfilled. This gave me an inner security . . . . Often I had the feeling that in all decisive matters I was no longer among men, but was alone with God." – C. G. Jung (1989, p. 48)

In chapters one through five we explored a new view of psychology based on teleological, fatalistic assumptions, and we examined the philosophical implications of adopting this perspective. We will now examine contemporary psychological research in light of this new meta-theory. The field of personality psychology has been embroiled in controversy over the past few decades; however, one emerging debate, important not only to personality psychologists, but which also has ramifications for all of psychology, is how the field should be structured. Arguably, personality psychologists are the most ambitious of psychologists in terms of the scope, range, and breadth of human behavior that we seek to explain. We therefore incorporate and must consider research from other fields, including neuroscience, cognitive, and social psychology. The traditional organizational structure has primarily been theoretical in nature; seminal textbooks such as Hall and Lindzey's (1957) *Theories of Personality* have defined how the field is conceptualized and taught. In this approach personality psychology is organized around each theorist (e.g., Freud, Jung, Maslow, etc.) or theory (e.g., psychoanalytic, humanistic, and so on). The result is a theoretically well-grounded approach. However, it has become increasingly difficult to incorporate contemporary research into this paradigm, predominantly because personality research is no longer driven by these grand theories. As a result, many textbooks read like historical accounts of psychology with significant omissions of recent developments in the field. Those who argue for abandoning this traditional approach offer alternatives, including the systems framework (Mayer, 2005), a "new big five" (McAdams & Pals, 2006), and the "tree of knowledge system" (Henriques, 2003). Each of the developments is impressive and worthy of investigation. The shortcoming with each contemporary development, however, is that, despite claims for unification and integration, they are merely "organizational frameworks." They do answer the important question of how to best organize and conceptualize information in psychology, but they fall short in content. Does any philosophical position unite all of psychology? What themes do we find that transcend and unite levels of analysis? And what do these themes say about what it means to be human?

I have attempted to elucidate a unified theory in the previous chapters. Many psychologists heartily resist discussion regarding our underlying assumptions because they categorize these issues as being within the domain of philosophy. However, our scientific method is based on philosophical positions that must be comprehended. The purpose of chapters six and seven is to integrate central areas of personality psychology into the meta-theory of the Moirae. Evolutionary psychology and psychoanalysis will be addressed in chapter six, because they analyze psychological mechanisms which operate predominantly beyond our conscious awareness, and both theories moreover make the boldest attempts to explain human nature. In particular, we compare the evolutionary perspective with the Moirae, since both are contemporary views regarding what it means to be human. Perspectives on personality that emphasize trait, cognitive, and humanist ideas, thus giving greater attention to individual differences in functioning rather than unconscious forces and theories of human nature, will be covered in chapter seven. Also in chapter seven is a discussion of narrative psychology which presents pivotal subjects for integration with the Moirae. I argued at the start that the topical theory of this book can serve as a meta-theory for all of psychology. One can therefore reasonably ask how this theory relates to other areas. My purpose in chapters six and seven is to review the key theoretical perspectives in personality psychology and show how we can reinterpret this data in a whole new light, a teleological light, that can unify and connect disparate areas of psychology.

Let us begin this reinterpretation by exploring the areas of psychology that are most conducive to a fatalistic position and act as precursors to the present theory. Much of psychoanalytic thought is historically consistent with the Moirae. Both Freud's emphasis on the biological drive that develops the personality and Jung's conceptualization of the collective unconscious contribute to a theoretical basis for the Moirae. The key distinction is drawn where the Moirae pulls us in particular directions based on a genetically based future oriented personal unconscious, while the psychoanalytic unconscious is a past determinant based on early experience. We will also examine Freud's Oedipus complex, Jung's collective unconscious, and Erikson's epigenetic principle in relation to the Moirae.

Psychoanalytic roots

The branch of psychology most implicitly receptive to fatalism is psychoanalysis. Many psychoanalysts would likely balk at such a notion. However, the romanticism surrounding psychoanalytic figures and ideas is far more extensive than in any other branch of psychology. At its core psychoanalysis attempts to develop empirical observation into a meaningful story about human personality (McAdams, 2001). This makes it fertile intellectual ground from which fatalistic psychology can spring. This section examines the fatalistic views and concepts found in the two towering figures in the psychoanalytic movement; that is, Sigmund Freud and Carl Jung.

As discussed in the previous chapter, Freud's psychology is rooted in biology and determinism. When studying Freud's theory of personality we often forget that he was trained in medicine and biology. As a young neurologist examining psychological disorders, he sought physical answers regarding the causes of neuroses. However, he and others were unable to locate physical causality. Only then did he turn to psychological explanations in his attempt to relate mental disturbance to human biology. In Freud's system biologically rooted instincts formed an energy system that gave rise to important personality determinants such as the unconscious, the id, complexes, and the libido, which operated outside of our awareness. Similarly, the Moirae are biologically rooted and operate on the unconscious level by pulling us in particular directions throughout our lives. However, Freud neither placed emphasis on the individual's lifelong developmental path that draws us toward a particular something, nor did he delineate our shared ancestry, as we see in the Moirae and in the work of Freud's protégé Carl Jung.

Jung presents an entirely different view of the unconscious than Freud, the foremost difference being the nature of the unconscious and the role of sexuality. Jung viewed sexuality as an important variable in the human experience, but certainly not the *prime* determinant of human behavior, as did Freud. More importantly, Jung not only emphasized a personal unconscious but he also viewed all humanity and life itself as related through what he coined as the *collective unconscious*. As Jung (1927/1971) states,

> The collective unconscious, however, as the ancestral heritage of possibilities of representations, is not individual but common to all men, and perhaps even to all animals, and is the true basis of the individual psyche. This whole psychic organism corresponds exactly to the body, which, though individually varied, is in all essential features the specifically human body which all men have. In its development and structure, it still preserves elements that connect it with the

invertebrates and ultimately with the protozoa (p. 38). The collective unconscious contains the whole spiritual heritage of mankind's evolution, born anew
in the brain structure of every individual (p. 45).

The collective unconscious is comprised of archetypes. Jung (1919/1971)
explains that ". . . in order to account for the uniformity and regularity of our
perceptions, we must have recourse to the correlated concept of a factor determining the mode of apprehension. It is this factor which I call the archetype or
primordial image" (p. 56). "Archetypes are typical modes of apprehension, and
wherever we meet with uniform and regularly recurring modes of apprehension
we are dealing with an archetype, no matter whether its mythological character
is recognized or not" (p. 57). In more familiar and contemporary language
McAdams (2001) describes them as, "inherited but somewhat flexible templates
for human experience. They are not images or behaviors as such but rather are
predispositions to develop universal images and to enact universal behavioral
sequences" (p. 133). Perhaps the best way to understand this important concept
is to examine two profound examples of archetypes and explain their relationship to the Moirae.

A classic example is that of the "mother" archetype. Infants inherit a predisposition to interpret experiences regarding a mother figure with prototypical
behaviors that transcend culture and time. This predisposition helps to shape the
infant's early interactions with and interpretations of the mother's behavior. Interaction between infant and biological mother is then molded in correspondence
with the archetype. Later in life the mother archetype may be expressed as symbols, stories, art, and so on. Another embedded archetype is the hero; narratives
highlight the protagonist who overcomes early struggles in order to battle enemy
forces, but who then experiences a downfall due to human fallibility. Joseph
Campbell (1949) has elaborated on the nature of the hero archetype and cited its
prominence in religious stories and mythologies across time and cultures. Jung's
archetypes resemble the Moirae in that they organize and direct the interpretations of our lives on an unconscious level and manifest in a variety of ways.
However, from a theoretic standpoint they are not teleologically-centered constructs, with one exception to be discussed later.

Archetypes can manifest as early *complexes* in the unconscious of children
which then act as causal forces that impact later adult interactions. Although
Freud rejected Jung's notion of a collective unconscious and archetypes, a long-
standing example is Freud's (1923/1961) Oedipal complex. Freud viewed human development as occurring through a series of psychosexual stages: the oral,
anal, phallic, latency, and genital stages with the core of personality being
formed at the end of the phallic stage by approximately age six. The central development during the latency stage is the resolution of the Oedipal complex. We
discussed the ancient Greek story of *Oedipus Rex* in chapter one where Oedipus
unwittingly murders his father and marries his mother. In a similar way, Freud
believed that beginning around age three or four boys unconsciously invest their
libido into making their mother into a love object while seeking to eliminate the
primary threat to this goal, that is, the boy's father. The anxiety produced by

these desires leads to the fear that the father will eliminate the boy's potential power by removing his penis, thus resulting in the child's sense of castration anxiety. Resolution of this conflict takes place when the boy begins to identify with his father and, through him, satisfies his desires vicariously. Freud viewed this psychodrama as universal and biologically rooted. The inability to adequately resolve this conflict according to Freud, can lead to a neurotic complex that causes problems in adulthood, including an inadequate moral structure, romantic difficulties, and/or problems with authority figures. However, considering Jung's views of archetypes and the Moirae, it may be better to view Freud's Oedipal complex as an archetype relative to many, but not all young children who love their mothers and are jealous of their father's intimacy with her. This archetype may manifest in play, fantasies, games, and stories. Furthermore, from the standpoint of the Moirae it may be that a biological disposition, the culture, and the home environment interact to unconsciously draw the young child into the Moirae of an Oedipal drama, whereby they are attracted to this fantasy and may seek to act it out through play. For example, some boys may enjoy play fighting with Dad and making proclamations about marrying Mom when they grow up. The unconscious attraction toward this archetype could then manifest itself throughout adult relationships and interpersonal dramas in numerous ways.

Henry Murray (1955) also identified an Icarus complex based on the Greek mythological figure who against his father's advice, flew too close to the sun with his wax wings and plunged to his death in the ocean below. Those suffering from an Icarus complex exhibit the following characteristics: narcissism, a desire for immortality, quashed ambitions, enuresis, and a cathexis for fire. Murray borrows the Icarus analogy to construct a coherent meaning around case studies of people who exhibited seemingly disparate psychological characteristics (McAdams, 2001). The Icarus complex could also be viewed as an archetype within Jungian psychology and a Moirae within the present discussion, whereby certain individuals are drawn toward seemingly disparate behaviors to fulfill a calling once manifest as an ancient myth. The elements and structure of this story serve to coordinate and direct these people's lives.

I would also offer what could be termed a Phoenix complex to help explain why certain individuals repeatedly reenact the process of birth, a spiraling toward death, and then rebirth. The Egyptian myth of the Phoenix relates the story of a bird that constructs a nest at the end of its life and sets it ablaze, reducing itself to ashes from which it is then reborn. This myth can serve as a basis for one type of manifestation of the Moirae of the circle that draws certain individuals toward this particular behavioral pattern. Examples cited in chapter three, especially in the case of drug/alcohol addiction, indicate that a person may be able to break free of this complex or to substitute increasingly productive behaviors for the destructive behaviors; one example is the religious "rebirth" and centering of life around religious ritual. The behavior is therefore changed and yet the Moirae of the circle still operate in the individual's life, but now manifest as different behaviors.

Jung's definition of the collective unconscious and archetypes are clear pre-cursors to my own conceptualization of the Moirae. Similar to the Moirae, there is strong emphasis in Jung's definition on a universal human connection that arises in the psychology of all life. Jung sees the foundations of personality emerging from an archaic, ancestral force that is biological and unconscious in nature. There is another key point of similarity between Jung's theory and the Moirae. Jung's theory is teleological with its emphasis on developmental aspirations, and can be seen precisely in his concept of individuation and the self.

In Jung's (1951/1971) view, the central archetype for understanding human personality is the self. The self is our life goal and is a unification of all parts of our personality. This striving for unification of the personality is a teleological view as opposed to the deterministic causal view of Freud. Not only are we driven by childhood complexes, but we are also pulled toward the full development of the self across our lives. Jung believes this personality development to be highlighted during mid-life where latent aspects of the personality now need to be integrated. This archetype of the holistic self is manifest in spiritual symbols like the mandala, and also in the process of alchemy carried out during the Middle Ages. The unity of the self can also be symbolized in archetypal lives like that of Christ or Buddha. We are called toward this unification of the self and it is the ultimate goal of life. Realization of the self appears through Jung's description of the *transcendent function*: the unification of a person's unconscious aspects and conscious processes, resulting in the development of the whole self. A similar understanding of how the Moirae operate in our lives enables us to exert greater control over our future.

In addition to the causal forces of the past and the teleological calling during our development, Jung (1955/1973) also recognized a third dynamic which he called *synchronicity*. He advanced this acausal concept to explain coincidences, in particular paranormal phenomena, which appear to be meaningful. Jung viewed the archetypes as responsible for our cognizance of meaningful connections in chance events. He conceptualized synchronicity as an "acausal orderedness." Obviously, one is then tempted to conclude that archetypes are the cause of the mental and physical coincidences. However, as Jung (1955/1973) states, " But as soon as he perceives the archetypal background he is tempted to trace the mutual assimilation of independent psychic and physical processes back to a (causal) effect of the archetype, and thus to overlook the fact that they are merely contingent. This danger is avoided if one regards synchronicity as a special instance of general acausal orderedness . . . for the archetype *is* the intro-spectively recognizable form of *a priori* psychic orderedness" (p. 100). We should also remember that Jung rooted the archetypes in our biological heritage while still maintaining that they are part of our psychological structure.

The archetypes therefore provide the link between physical and mental co-incidence in an acausal manner. Jung's concept is difficult to comprehend and not as intuitive as causal principles of explanation; nevertheless it is a superior position to that of an intangible mind that somehow magically manipulates the physical world. More importantly, it provides us with an analogy regarding how the Moirae may operate within our lives aside from teleology or causality. The concept of synchronicity also elucidates how an unconscious process, like the Moirae, can shape our lives while still allowing for the opportunities of free will explored in chapter five.

Similar to Jung's conceptualization of the self is Erikson's *epigenetic principle*. Erikson proposed that we undergo eight developmental stages, each corresponding to a particular age period. The teleological force which propels us through these eight developmental stages is the epigenetic principle. Erikson (1980) states " . . . that anything that grows has a *ground plan*, and that out of this ground plan the *parts* arise, each part having its *time* of ascendancy, until all parts have arisen to form a *functioning whole*" (p. 53). It is tenable from his definition that we are drawn toward a particular life goal embedded in our biological development. Psychologically, Erikson believes that we are drawn toward the virtue of wisdom in the "Integrity versus Despair" end stage of our life. In both theories of Jung and Erikson we see an unfolding of biologically-based life, similar to the hatching of an egg, or a flower in bloom. Environmental conditions are essential for this development, but the teleological purpose resident in our lives is housed in our biology. In a similar way, we see that our Moirae call us toward a particular life path.

Finally, there is one aspect of Freud's theory that could be interpreted from a teleological perspective, despite the fact that he uses language to develop a causal, deterministic interpretation. Freud's discussion of the instincts in *Beyond the Pleasure Principle* (1920/1995) and *The Ego and the Id* (1923/1961) provides a fascinating window into Freud's desire to link psychological processes with the physical world. Freud generally divides human instincts into two main categories, that of Eros, which includes all the life instincts, and Thanatos, all the death instincts. Eros includes the libido, or sex drive, and is primarily responsible for our biological desire to procreate, which Freud deduced as the basis for much of psychological life. Freud extensively elaborated the nature of the libido, since it represented the foundation for the psychosexual stages and the structure of personality in his theory. More interestingly for our purposes here, he also provides a fascinating analysis of the origin of the death instinct, which includes aggressive urges, in *Beyond the Pleasure Principle*; he notes in his work that all life evolved from an inorganic form and the first instances of life were brief and devolved back into that form relatively quickly. Biological life gradually gained a strong foothold, not only by being able to sustain itself, but also to successfully reproduce. Freud asserts that this evolution from inorganic to biological life is the basis of the death instinct. What is very interesting about this discussion is his emphasis on the "conservative" nature of this (and all) instincts driving us toward a previous state of existence. For Freud to keep his theoretical system intact it was necessary for him to view the death instinct within a homeostatic interpretation.

However, when we envision Eros and Thanatos through the Moirae we can make a very different, teleological interpretation. What we see from the biological evidence is a constant "calling" toward life and non-life. The Moirae of the universe drew inorganic matter into an organic form eventually establishing reproductive life. At the same time, we are called toward an inorganic state, not in a conservative or regressive manner, but drawn toward the "home" of an inorganic state. Freud (1920/1995) came close to this view when he stated that "the aim of all life is death" (p. 613); what he failed to acknowledge is that the aim of all death is life. The Moirae of life and death each act as an attractive force in our lives and manifest themselves in our consciousness and behaviors as we saw in chapter two.

The most serious problem with the psychoanalytic approach is its primary emphasis on past determinism. For Freud, our present behavior and thought are always driven by past conflicts. For Jung, the nature of the unconscious differs, but his emphasis on past determinism is nevertheless retained. In a way, Jung even extends the notion by implying through the collective unconscious that our behavior is even influenced by human history. For the Moirae, dynamic motivation is the result of the future not the past because it is primarily a teleologically-rooted theory. In psychoanalytic theory, dynamic, motivational constructs push us forward. Instead I am proposing that we are *pulled* or drawn toward the future by the dynamic, motivational forces of the Moirae. Jung does, however, indicate how archetypes can operate in a teleological function through his explanation of the self and the process of individuation. And, we see that although Jung and Erikson's theories are slightly rooted in teleology, the implications of it are not thoroughly elucidated and seem secondary to the concepts and structure defined within the theories of personality. The Moirae, however, emphasizes the foremost role that the future, personal unconscious plays in drawing us to particular life paths. We are also more easily able to integrate the role of free will into the human experience, contrary to deterministic theory, as we described in chapter five.

Evolutionary psychology

The research conducted in more contemporary fields such as neuroscience and evolutionary psychology is also consistent with a fatalistic position. These fields adopt a Nativistic philosophy whereby the psychological and biological constitution of the person constrains human choice. Furthermore, these constraints operate outside of conscious awareness. These points are most clearly illustrated when the Moirae, and these subdisciplines of psychology, address issues such as aggression, religious behaviors, gender, sexuality, and social hierarchies.

Evolutionary psychologists examine how the process of natural selection has shaped the commonalities in human personality that transcend time and culture. At first glance, evolutionary psychology and psychoanalysis do not seem to share much in common. However, we can observe two fundamental philosophical postulates that the fields share not only with each other but also with the Moirae. First, both psychoanalysis and evolutionary psychology are rooted in the broad biological basis of behavior. As we have just seen, many psychoanalytic ideas are embedded in the biology of human beings. Second, researchers in both fields agree that common human ancestry contributes to current behavior. In psychoanalysis, this ancestry manifests as the unconscious. For evolutionary psychologists it results in an emphasis on what have been called distal predictors of behavior, which are contrasted with proximate predictors. This distinction is critical to our understanding of how evolutionary processes impact on human nature and individual differences (Wright, 1994). *Proximate* predictors refer to the immediate motivational, situational, cognitive, developmental, and physiological reasons for why a person engages in a behavior. *Distal* predictors explain behavioral patterns which have had an evolutionary advantage, especially at the group level. The process of natural selection acts as a distal predictor that helps to explain human nature and individual differences (Buss, 1997). Ultimately, human biology has developed such that the successful genetic replication is highest. Our biology, therefore, is the product of what Richard Dawkins (1976) has metaphorically labeled "the selfish gene"; our behavior maximizes the success of our genes' reproduction. Evolutionary psychologists have shown that the result of this design places powerful constraints upon our behavior and guides our behaviors in particular directions that foster genetic replication. These random contingencies placed on human behavior are an excellent example of how the Moirae manifest itself through our biology.

It is crucial at this point to notice an implicit assumption found in evolutionary psychology. There is an inherent deterministic and mechanistic model at work when we discuss distal predictors. The assumption behind this biological model is that genes "cause" events to transpire and therefore are the distal reason for our behaviors. However, we have yet to unearth discussion regarding a teleological view of how genes operate. Let us consider that genes are the physical manifestations of our fate. For example, is not the "groundwork" for an apple tree already contained in the apple seed? The genes in each seed, along with the proper environment, aid in the fulfillment of its destiny. However, the destiny was already inherent in the seed before the tree even existed. As we review the evolutionary literature let us interpret the data through the lens of the Moirae. Notice that the findings in evolutionary psychology are consistent with the Moirae as has been delineated in preceding chapters.

The reason the data is not typically interpreted within a teleological and fatalistic framework is due to the non-empirical assumptions behind evolutionary psychology that rely on an outdated, mechanistic world view. I believe that the Moirae show us that we are being pulled toward our fate through our genes; instead of viewing the genes as a past causal agent "pushing" us toward behaviors (although this may be partially true). One can easily interpret the research findings in a teleological framework and argue that genes draw us toward particular behaviors. Let us consider the following analogy: A girl plans to clear away the snow on her driveway. She moves the shovel in systematic paths or rows, until the snow is gone. Now imagine an observer who can see everything except the shovel and the girl. The observer argues that the systematic movement and accumulation of each particle of snow has pushed the snow behind it (which is true). However, the observer misses the purposive agent existing be-

hind the event, that is, the girl shoveling the snow! It was the girl who envi-
sioned a clear driveway and performed the action necessary to fulfill the task.

In the same way, the universe has an unfolding purpose and direction that is
manifested in physical form (and by implication something must be pulling us in
that direction). In the case of evolutionary psychology, the physical form which
is the key mechanism of transformation is the gene. However, the unseen hand
of the Moirae operates behind this physical description exactly as the girl and
her shovel. As the apple tree is already contained in the seed, so do our genes
already contain our destiny. However, a byproduct of our physical development
is consciousness which paradoxically allows us to potentially deviate from our
destiny. We keep this in mind as we explore how evolutionary psychologists
explain the origins of human behavior.

Evolutionary psychologists place great emphasis on the environment where
human beings have lived for most of their time on earth—Environment of Evolutionary Adaptedness—often referred to as the (EEA) and corresponds to the
two million years in which we lived in nomadic, cooperative, small groups as
hunters and gatherers (Bowlby, 1969). The millions of years spent in this environment have produced similarities across cultures that manifest themselves in
universal behaviors and customs that now transcend time and place. These patterns are now a part of our genetic structure (Wilson, 1978) and as a result are
our shared Moirae, thus constituting part of our genetically inherited collective
unconscious. Furthermore, this environment has produced in humans a "cognitive niche" (Pinker, 1997). According to this view, due to natural selection humans have developed a vast array of specialized thinking patterns (cognitive
abilities) which allow them to adapt and change their environments (Buss, 1997;
Pinker, 1997). The large number of innate cognitive mechanisms, according to
Buss (1997), has actually led to greater human flexibility and adaptation. On
average then, humans are capable of solving a multitude of problems thanks to
the wide array of cognitive specializations in the brain, thereby increasing the
chances of genetic replication at the aggregate group level.

Let us now examine the variety of ways that these genetic enticements form
patterns of behaviors that we can categorize as part of the Moirae. Each of the
following areas of research within evolutionary psychology illustrates how our
genes pull us toward particular behavioral patterns. When we examine eating
behavior, sexuality, aggression, altruism, social hierarchies, and religion we not
only see commonalities across cultures and time because of natural selection,
but we also see the hand of unconscious forces that draws us toward particular
life paths.

Most of us think that eating behaviors are the product of our personal
choices and so our weight is a direct result of making choices. However, the
research in evolutionary psychology, neuroscience, and nutrition sciences shows
that this is a highly inaccurate picture. From an evolutionary vantage point a diet
rich in sugars, salt, and fat in the EEA gave humans a greater chance of survival
for millions of years, as did the ability to store energy through fat (Pinel, 2006).
Furthermore, in a food scarce environment such as the EEA it was important to

consume large amounts of food when it was available. The result of the natural selection process over millions of years is that we are not only predisposed to particular tastes but also to the consumption of large amounts of food at one time. The reasons for this advantage are obvious in the nomadic, hunter-gatherer societies of the EEA where nutrient-rich foods were sporadically available. However, the tendency to consume large amounts in an environment replete with salty, fat-saturated, and sugar-rich foods contributes largely to the health problems seen in some modern societies. Furthermore, recent research (see Pinel, 2006) reveals genetic individual differences in how food is stored and metabolized. Finally, there are a host of cultural traditions in Western society (particularly in the United States) which further exacerbate the problem, including desk jobs, consumption of three large meals a day, and the inclusion of food at nearly every social gathering (Pinel, 2006). We therefore see strong biological and cultural forces attracting us to particular foods, and we are exposed to culturally-prescribed eating practices beginning early in our lives. These biological, social, cultural, and historical factors that shape our eating behaviors are products of our fate and another important manifestation of the Moirae in our lives.

We have cursorily examined the Moirae of human sexuality in chapter two. Evolutionary psychologists have much to contribute to our discussion when we examine general gender differences in sexual behaviors and cognitions (Buss, 1991; Wright, 1994). Genetically speaking and at the aggregate level, the EEA selected different mating strategies which were most effective for each gender. In order to procreate it is optimal for males to impregnate as many females as possible since the act of copulation is the minimal physiological requirement. Females are meanwhile biologically prescribed to invest more time and physiological resources into each birth, thus resulting in a more selective strategy for mating. Obviously, there are tremendous individual differences among members of each sex; however, at the distal level of explanation, consistent aggregate differences in male and female sexual behaviors (that transcend culture and time) are evident and explicable through evolutionary processes. These biological forces often then shape and reinforce cultural norms which provide the social, moral, and religious regulations with reference to these behaviors. The results are differences in motivation, fantasy, and behavior of males and females regarding sexuality. A husband may only engage in sexual behavior with his wife through most or all of his life; however, even for these faithful males, the Moirae of sexuality manifest in their unrequited desires and fantasies. Even in the case of males who choose not to engage in sexual relations for religious reasons, celibacy is often a particularly difficult challenge. The selectivity of females is also accompanied by comparatively less emphasis on the physical appearance of the male and greater concern with the male's resources and power which are important determinants for protecting her "genetic investment." Therefore, the female may marry the young man her own age who does not have access to wealth and power, but she may nevertheless fantasize about a "prince" taking her away or a "sugar daddy" meeting all of her needs. We must remember that genetic variation, social upbringing, cultural diversity, and personal preference contribute to a much wider range of sexual attitudes and behaviors than is indicated in the evolutionary explanation. However, the Moirae of each gender's relationship to his or her sexuality is still expressed through the person's biology and the cultural ideals to which they are exposed.

Two seemingly opposite human behaviors, that is, aggression and altruism, are also influenced by evolutionary heritage and in turn provide various incentives through the Moirae. The ancient Greeks recognized that aggression was endemic to the human condition and classic works such as *The Iliad* and *The Odyssey* memorably portray these characteristics. Furthermore, we find tributes to aggression and war throughout human history and across many cultures (although not universally). Evolutionary psychologists also emphasize the adaptive significance (particularly for males) of aggression in the EEA which leads to a predisposition toward intraspecies aggression. Furthermore, our aggression is often intricately related to other evolutionary influenced behaviors including group identification, jealousy, and the social hierarchy. Altruistic behavior, meanwhile, is most often displayed toward family members and especially children. It is also intricately intertwined with group dynamics, interpersonal and familial relations, and the social hierarchy. The example of parental love most easily conforms to the evolutionary psychologists' ideas regarding human behaviors, cognitions, and emotions being the products of "selfish genes." We are drawn toward aggression through the Moirae to protect and provide resources for our family and tribe, but these same forces also compel us toward the love and protection experienced with friends and family.

Human social structure in the EEA was hierarchically organized with an emphasis placed on social status within the hierarchy. This organizational pattern remains the case in most instances in contemporary society (Wright, 1994). Hierarchical patterns of organization are found in mammalian societies and humanity is no exception. Status within the hierarchy is expressed through gestures, symbols, titles, etc. and is found within almost every organization in society, including families, schools, businesses, and governments. Status may be gained through physical aggression or the threat of such action. However, in adult human relationships it is a more complicated and malleable concept than seen in other animals. For example, within the family or work environments the status hierarchy can shift according to the task or the issue the group is addressing.

The famous obedience studies of Stanley Milgram (1974) serve to illustrate the powerful influence of our social hierarchies. Milgram constructed an experimental procedure whereby participants were led to believe that they were shocking another participant to the point of serious pain and even jeopardizing the participant's life. However, no painful shocks were administered. Contrary to Milgram's intuition, he found that most of his participants were willing to continue giving (albeit reluctantly) electric shocks despite strong evidence that they were seriously harming another human being. Subsequent obedience studies over the past few decades confirm and extend Milgram's original findings, thus indicating that our tendency to obey authority is one of the most powerful situational determinants we face—with our attitudes, morals, personality variables, and gender serving as inferior predictors of behavior in hierarchically-organized social structures. One only need observe the course of human history to see how the power of obedience to authority has accomplished both the most horrific and heroic acts. Furthermore, the social hierarchies in which we often find ourselves are rarely the products of our free choices but more often are subject to our fate.

Social psychologists are not the only researchers to have examined the powerful situational determinants that highlight the role of status and hierarchy. Personality researchers too have identified a particular dispositional trait whereby an individual's emphasis on authority can be measured. Most of us exhibit moderate levels of authoritarianism. However, there is a subset of humans who have been labeled authoritarians who have an excessive adherence to conventional norms, an overweening inclination to have an uncritical stance toward authority, and who express aggression toward those who do not fit comfortably within the sanctioned conventional hierarchy (Altemeyer, 1981, 1988). The roots of authoritarianism may be, at least partially, unconscious (Adorno, Frenkel-Brunswick, Levinson, & Sanford, 1950). Furthermore, this personality variable has been shown to be adaptive from an evolutionary perspective (Hastings & Shaffer, in press) and that the tendency to ascribe to authoritarian attitudes increases in response to threat (Doty, Peterson, & Winter, 1991; McCann & Stewin, 1987; Feldmen & Stenner, 1997; Hastings & Shaffer, 2005; Shaffer & Hastings, 2004).

What does the evidence from evolutionary psychology in the examination of social hierarchies, the social psychology studies of obedience, and the personality studies of authoritarianism reveal about the Moirae? Here we see evidence of how biologically-based behaviors are expressed in our culture, social structures, and personalities to draw us toward behaviors that ultimately emphasize submission and conformity within a social hierarchy with sanctioned rules on how to gain status within it. The evidence shows that these forces are powerful in our everyday lives; research moreover indicates that these forces work outside of our conscious awareness. I teach at least one section of social psychology each year. The focus of the course is how social situations and personality variables dictate most of our behavior on a daily basis. Each time I teach the class, students comment on how they see the world differently and that they had never realized how much of their behavior was automatic. Indeed, I had a similar experience as an undergraduate. In these cases, we find that knowledge of the Moirae can potentially increase the possibilities for free will. The social psychology research confirms this notion. Researchers have shown that those who become aware of influential situational determinants and automatic thinking patterns are less likely to fall prey to the pitfalls of these phenomena (Cialdini, 2001).

We also find that evolutionary psychology has much to contribute regarding our understanding of religious behavior. Religion has provided two essential psychological dimensions, among others, to our existence that has proven to be evolutionarily advantageous. First, a spiritual sensibility helps to cement our identification with the group; this identification process in the EEA and today provides protection and sustenance (Wilson, 1978; Wright, 1994). Bonds are often forged through elaborate and sacred rituals that reinforce the social hierarchy and tie the members together toward a common purpose (Newberg et al., 2001). Furthermore, researchers in social psychology have found that our social identities not only help to formulate a sense of self but also direct our relations toward those outside the group (Tajfel, 1978). Second, our ties to the group are solidified through the life meaning and purpose that the religion provides (Wilson, 1978). Moral codes are most often directly related not only to religious beliefs but also to individuals who operate as functionaries within the religious order and are deemed especially able to sanction correct moral conduct. De Waal (1996) demonstrates that, across cultures, moral codes exhibit common prescriptions for behavior that are related to survival in the EEA, including an emphasis on, norm-related social rules, reciprocity, empathy, and communal values when resolving conflicts.

It is interesting to note that these values, as extensions of religious beliefs, are also found to be powerful situational determinants in the social psychology literature; not only do we find that studies on obedience and authoritarianism solidify the evolving social hierarchy, but that outcomes in conformity and social norms also demonstrate the overwhelming power of group consensus. Perhaps the most famous research in this area is that of Solomon Asch (1956). In a series of studies, participants were asked to select which line most closely approximated a standard comparison line. Alone, the participants were accurate 99% of the time. However, another group of participants were placed in a group of confederates who colluded with the experimenter to provide unanimously wrong answers to prearranged comparison cards. What Asch found surprised even him; 76% of the participants provided the conforming, incorrect response on at least one occasion. In other words, people were willing to publicly state an answer that they knew was wrong in order to conform to the group. Subsequent research confirms Asch's initial findings that conformity pressures are overwhelming and occur in a variety of everyday settings. Furthermore, these pressures increase as the strength of our identification with the group increases. Friends and families appear to provide the strongest conformity pressures; this is consistent with evolutionary psychology analyses. Furthermore, we find that religious structures most often work in combination with familial pressures to reinforce identity and compliance to the prescribed moral framework. At birth we find ourselves thrown into a familial, social, and religious structure that immediately begins to exert implicit and explicit conformity pressures. Here we see the Moirae operating on a quotidian basis through social institutions, its pressures of which we are only vaguely aware.

Conclusions

As we end this chapter we can more clearly delineate the commonalities we see between psychoanalysis, evolutionary psychology, and the Moirae. From a historical perspective it is clear that Darwin's theory of evolution influenced both Freud's and Jung's ideas. Freud's central concept of an Eros operating outside conscious awareness is directly related to Darwin's ideas regarding instinctual behavior and survival. The Darwinian influence is perhaps most pronounced in Jung's theory of the collective unconscious. Jung's emphasis on heredity and the ancestral, experiential quality of archetypes within the collective unconscious puts him in the contemporarily awkward position of adopting the doctrine of acquired characteristics which is inconsistent with modern biology. However, we can also view the collective unconscious and archetypes as a product of natural selection. In other words, instead of early ancestral experiences being inherited, it may be that individuals with certain cognitive predispositions had a greater facility to adapt within the EEA. As a result, all humans now share inherent neurological predispositions that influence how we interpret and construct reality. Furthermore, we find that once again our fate is rooted in our biological heritage and is then expressed in our psychology, social situations, societal institutions, and culture.

Aside from the historical influence of evolutionary theory on theorists such as Freud and Jung, we also find a haunting similarity between contemporary evolutionary psychology and the theories of Freud and Jung. In both examples of classic psychoanalysis and evolutionary psychology we see a theoretical perspective that, while emphasizing human biology and instincts, results in discussions of spirituality, religion, and morality. In the same way that Freud and Jung wrote extensively on these issues, evolutionary psychologists have also increasingly focused on them. In Freud's early writings he discussed the growth of the superego and morality from our instinctual id. His later works are predominantly discussions of the origins of God and morality in human psychology (e.g., *The Future of an Illusion, Moses and Monotheism*, and *Civilization and its Discontents*). Jung's works exhibit a consistent concern with how the paranormal, religious iconography and spirituality relate to human psychology. Similarly, evolutionary psychologists have focused on morals (de Waal, 1996; Wright, 1994) and religion (Dawkins, 2006; Wilson, 1978). Clearly one reason for this similarity is the scope and ambition of the theories. As Buss (1999) has recognized, each theory is a "grand theory" of personality; that is, a theory that attempts to describe human nature and the reasons for individual differences. This is undoubtedly true. However, I believe that each theory has stumbled across these issues because they are both linked in the Moirae. Each theory asserts that biology and psychology are the basis of religion and morality. Furthermore, I propose that, through the Moirae, our biology operates as a vehicle for the development of consciousness, which in turn yields our psychology and morality. This distinction is crucial. In both Freud (far less so in Jung) and contemporary evolutionary psychologists, religion, spirituality, and morality are byproducts or even epiphenomena of deterministic biological and psychological functioning. This is not true from the perspective of the Moirae. When we see human development through a teleological lens whereby our future, personal unconscious pulls us along our life path, we see that we are made *from* the physical universe *for* consciousness, freedom, spirituality, morality, and religion. Evolutionary psychologists, who assert that consciousness, free will, spirituality, morality, and religion are the result of biological evolution, are patently oblivious to destiny. Freud's argument that the morality of the superego is some sort of perversion of biological instincts, or that God is an illusion based on psychological needs, misses our true nature. As the Greeks showed how fate spawns both the best and worst of humanity in their poetry, plays, and mythology, we now see how our physical existence and social contingencies give rise to the flowers of human existence. Our biology, culture, and history are the soil from which our consciousness generates free will, spirituality, morality, and religion.

Chapter 7

Can People Change? Stories, Traits, and Clinical Applications

"We do not inherit personality traits or even behavior mechanisms as such. What is inherited are chemical templates that produce and regulate proteins involved in building the structure of nervous systems and the neurotransmitters, enzymes, and hormones that regulate them. We are not born extraverts, neurotics, impulsive, sensation seekers, or antisocial personalities, but we are born with differences in reactivities of brain structures and levels of regulators like MAO. How do these differences in biological traits shape our choices in life from the manifold possibilities provided by the environments?"
–Morton Zuckerman (1995, pp. 331-32)

As previously mentioned, our purpose in chapters six and seven is to reinterpret personality psychology in the teleological light of the Moirae. We have seen how psychoanalysis and evolutionary psychology can be incorporated into a fatalistic framework. We can now examine personality theories that emphasize individual differences in functioning such as the trait, cognitive, and humanistic perspectives. I will also discuss narrative psychology which presents some compelling areas for comparison with the Moirae. When reviewing these areas of psychology we encounter the following questions: How is character formed? Can people change? Do people change? By drawing from trait psychology research, the narrative approach, the humanistic approach, and various cognitive constructs, we will examine the influence of the Moirae on personality. In particular, I will devote attention to how trait psychology is grounded in a biological understanding of personality. The various philosophical conceptualizations of traits and the implications of these positions will be analyzed. For example, if mental health practitioners adopt a genetic, deterministic position in regard to traits, then how does this influence their approach toward client diagnosis and treatment, as well as affect their larger view of the human condition? Is the individual able to act inconsistently with his or her trait structure? The Moirae, meanwhile, allow for new interpretations of trait research. Similarly, research that employs a narrative approach to the comprehension of personality is consistent with the Moirae, in that narrative life structures often appear as particular forms relating to specific *archetypes* or story structures. Finally, in this chapter we will apply these ideas to the area of mental health care by discussing techniques for personal growth and change.

Traits

We have explored how psychoanalytic and evolutionary theories provide fertile soil for a fatalistic psychology. On closer examination, almost all theories of personality implicitly adopt a fatalistic perspective. However, because of the biases and prejudices previously mentioned in chapters one and two, many contemporary theorists are reluctant to extend the theories to their logical conclusion. One purpose of this chapter is to illustrate how contemporary personality theories, specifically trait, cognitive, humanistic, and narrative approaches, are explained and unified through an understanding of the Moirae.

The trait approach to understanding human behavior begins with the assumption that an internal disposition is the cause of behavior. For example, I will categorize someone as "extraverted" if I observe that person engaging in friendly, gregarious, and enthusiastic behavior. If I meet someone who expresses anxiety, self-consciousness, impulsivity, and depression then I will label the person "neurotic." Gordon Allport (1937) was the first of the contemporary psychologists to systematically organize the trait approach; he conceived that traits (1961) have a "neuropsychic structure." Drawn from the structure of language, Allport's analysis is known as the *lexical hypothesis.* Goldberg (1981, 1990) also noted that language patterns unveil everyday personality differences. Personality researchers therefore sought to discover the relevant dimensions of individual differences existing in natural language. The use of a statistical technique (i.e., factor analysis) by Cattell (1945) to determine universal trait structures ushered in an era where psychologists could attempt to mathematically uncover our trait structure. Numerous researchers have, in the past few decades, systematically utilized this factor analytic approach (Costa & McCrae, 1992; Goldberg, 1981, 1990; Norman, 1963; Tupes & Cristal, 1961). There were disagreements during this era on how to label each factor, and dispute as well about the actual number of important variables. However, the majority of personality researchers eventually decided upon five core traits. Costa and McCrae (1992) have been the leading advocates of what has become known as the Five-Factor Model (FFM). In this model, the traits of Extraversion, Neuroticism, Openness to Experience, Agreeableness, and Conscientiousness are viewed as the core trait structure of personality. Furthermore, most adherents to the FFM assume that traits are rooted in human biology (e.g., see Allport, 1937; Eysenk, 1967; McCrae & Costa, 1990; Zuckerman, 1991). Despite disagreement regarding the most important traits, most researchers unanimously agree that extraversion and neuroticism are the most important (McAdams, 2001). We will therefore focus on how the two traits relate to a fatalistic psychology. In truth, we could randomly pick any trait because the following argument is applicable to merely the *idea* of a trait.

Finding a biological cause for the complex array of behaviors comprising extraversion is not as simple as Allport once envisaged; where would we find specific biological agents responsible for the trait? Keep in mind that we are speaking of a diverse group of correlated behaviors including positive affect, excitement seeking, active lifestyle, assertiveness, gregariousness, and warmth (Costa & McCrae, 1992). We cannot simply locate a gene or group of genes that dictate an extraverted or introverted personality. Instead we find a complex array of genetic structures which influence our initial biology at birth; our biological self then proceeds to interact with our immediate environment. Gray (1987) has argued for a *behavioral approach system* (BAS) present in the biological constitution of those who score high on measures of extraversion. The hypothetical system BAS represents various neurological functions and primarily homes in on how we are motivated toward behavior, achieving goals, and positive emotional states. An important neurotransmitter in the BAS is dopamine; specifically, the functions of this neurotransmitter in the limbic system of the brain. Dopaminergic neural pathways in the limbic region relate directly to individual differences in reward-seeking behavior. Research also indicates that left anterior regions of the cerebral cortex may also be relevant to aspects of extraversion.

The case for neuroticism is similar. Neuroticism also encompasses a wide array of behaviors including anxiety, anger, depression, self-consciousness, impulsivity, and vulnerability (Costa & McCrae, 1992). Researchers (e.g., Le Doux, 1992) have explained our propensity toward neuroticism through a hypothesized biological structure identified as the behavioral inhibition system (BIS). Those high in neuroticism are vigilant to perceptions of danger, threat, or novelty, which in turn can cause a person to withdraw from the pursuit of a goal if he or she suspects negative emotional punishment. The biological substrate associated with such behaviors is the amygdala, which in many species regulates the fear response and so is included as one biological component in the BIS. Let us be clear here. In the case of the BAS and the BIS we are referring to a hypothesized biological system that has not yet been specifically delineated. The details regarding important structures, neurotransmitters, and functions are therefore sketchy. However, the research conducted thus far presents a strong case for biological predispositions and correlates with extraversion and neuroticism.

Furthermore, Daniel Nettle (2006) asserts that each of the traits in the five-factor model can also be integrated into an evolutionary framework. Genetic variation along personality variables provides adaptability and inclusive fitness because of the different costs and benefits regarding the behaviors associated with the spectrum of each variable. Therefore, in the case of extraversion and neuroticism we find that neither side of the spectrum is always advantageous (or

disadvantageous) to survival; adaptability is contingent on situation, and therefore genetic variability remains.

The question now arises, why are we born this way? Morton Zuckerman's
quote at the introduction of this chapter attempts to specify the nature of traits by
not reducing them to an essentialist character that waits passively for this or that
gene to be actualized, but rather by relating traits to biological dispositions.
Nevertheless, a biological or even genetic explanation is incomplete and any
search for a past cause is misguided. Instead, we should view these biological
predispositions as manifestations of our future destiny. The very word "disposition," which psychologists readily employ, suggests future causality. Our
Moirae lay in our biology, predisposing us to "choose" certain careers, friends,
mates, activities, etc. in our lifetime. In the same way that the genetic composition of an apple seed is the blue print of an apple tree, providing that it has an
adequate environment, our Moirae pulls us toward a particular destiny.

Controversy regarding the "components" of traits like extraversion and neuroticism is also misguided. Our Moirae through our biological inheritance estab-
lishes our general path. Along the way we accumulate different experiences. For
example, high correlations between extraversion and positive affect indicate that
different extraverts accumulate different experiences, but not that the positive
affect is necessarily a component of extraversion (McAdams, 2001). Extraversion is an aspect of one's Moirae that is expressed differently by each person.
Our biological predispositions manifest as traits prepare us to interpret events in
particular ways. For example, an introvert may have many opportunities to engage in social interactions, but the research suggests that introverts are more
likely to interpret social interactions negatively because they consider the punitive aspects of the interaction (e.g., interpersonal disagreements) than do most
extraverts (Cooper & Sealise, 1974; Norman & Watson, 1976). Such evidence
suggests that positive emotions are central to extraversion. However, other research suggests that positive emotions may not be central to extraversion (e.g.,
Matthews & Deary, 1998). Therefore, we see that extraversion is a useful hypothetical (even Platonic) construct that reflects a complex array of biological predispositions. However, the traits themselves are expressed uniquely by each
person. For one extravert, excitement seeking and activity may be chiefly emphasized, whereas for another warmth and gregariousness are predominant.
More important, the concept "extravert," representing complex biological predispositions, is contextualized within the individual's greater personality, circumstances, and environment. The result is that no two extraverts are alike.
Only with aggregate data across many people are we able to discern individual
differences along this dimension. But the role of extraversion at a personal level
depends upon the person's larger Moirae in forming their destiny. Our discussion of traits mirrors issues already outlined in chapter four in regard to Plato's
forms and the Moirae.

We are now at a critical point in our discussion: traits are not us; nor do
they define our nature. We are not merely a complex array of traits that represent biological predispositions. Earlier theorists like Allport tried to make a
similar point by distinguishing between nomothetic and idiographic research;

the former focusing on general principles across individuals, and the latter addressing the uniqueness of the individual. Since the early days of psychology, critics have argued that traits are tautological, in that they are labels and classifications of behaviors rather than explanations for behavior. For example, behaviorists consistently leveled these critiques against trait theory in the middle of the 20th century and warned of the dangers of reification. B.F. Skinner attempted to eliminate all intervening, hypothetical constructs, including traits, for explaining behavior. Recent tautological critiques are more sophisticated and have specifically addressed the five-factor model. Quackenbush (2001) argues that our observation of the stability of traits' expressions across time is a pre-empirical assumption of the theory, which essentially places the theory outside the realm of scientific inquiry, since such an assumption is not testable. Furthermore, I have argued that the five-factor model is representative of a heuristic metaphor that allows psychologists to communicate about abstract, functional concepts which are descriptive rather than causal taxonomy (Hastings, 2007).

Our discussion leads us to the conclusion that traits are not essence. Traits, traditionally conceptualized, or conceptualized through cognitive or humanistic approaches, are at heart, intellectual manifestations of attempts to construct meaning from existence. In the same way that adolescents identify with pop figures or fundamentalists have an affinity with religious figures or readings, trait psychologists construct meaning through psychological concepts. Therefore, advocates for traits will argue that we *are* extraverted, neurotic, conscientious, and so on. Our being becomes filled with a "concrete" essence that explains what we are. The Moirae, however, avoid what Sartre labeled our "bad faith" attempt to fill an existential vacuum.

Of course there is the possibility that the Moirae will be misinterpreted as a replacement for traits designated to also fill this void, but that would be a mistaken notion. The Moirae exist outside of us and are manifested through us; they connect us to the physical world and are also the springboard for consciousness. I am able to sidestep dualism here because both are ultimately intertwined. Our destiny draws us toward the future because of its relationship to the universe. The Moirae are the chemistry, physics, and biology of the universe. The neurochemical structures present early in our brain development are not us, nor are our parents us. These Moirae may pull us in a particular direction or lead us to a certain path. Ultimately, however, we cannot pull these Moirae into us and make them our essence, because our essence is a vacuum; it is our consciousness. That is the nature of free will. If we were able to explain what we truly are, our potential for free will would cease to exist. The Moirae pull us toward our destiny, but as free, moral agents we choose whether to accept it or not.

Cognitive and Humanistic Variables

We have thus far focused on traits, as trait theory is currently predominant in the personality psychology field. As a result, cognitive and humanistic psychologists tend to examine personality from an individual difference perspective. Social-cognitive and humanistic variables are not typically labeled as traits since they are chiefly characterized by motivational desires. Instead, these variables are known as *Personal Action Constructs* (Little, 1999) and *characteristic adaptations* (McAdams, 2001; McAdams & Pals, 2006). Theorists with a cognitive orientation note the significance of variables such as life tasks, personal projects, social schemata, personal strivings, and others. Individual difference variables have a distinct advantage over traditional traits, in that these cognitive variables emphasize the future; this allows for a thorough examination of the role of free will, due to the weight given to motivational aspects. There has moreover been less research examining biological correlates of these variables. It is interesting to note that motivational constructs with a cognitive emphasis are consistent with a teleological theory emphasizing fatalism.

Let us examine how three of these motivational variables with a cognitive emphasis stand out in the literature as exceptionally relevant to the Moirae. *Life tasks* are self-defined problems to which we devote significant resources when organizing our daily routines; they usually relate to a particular developmental period (Cantor & Zirkel, 1990). Emmons (1992) defines *personal strivings* as relatively continuous and stable goals across the life span. And third, Little (1989) views *personal projects* as short-term or long-term sequential activities directed toward a personal goal. There is obviously substantial conceptual overlap among them; each addresses purposive, conscious, goal-oriented behavior that involves problem solving. Notice how these variables nicely exemplify the free behavior borne of consciousness discussed in chapter five. Without life tasks, personal strivings, personal projects, or similar products of our free consciousness, we would truly be at the mercy of the whims of our fate. By developing purposive, goal-oriented plans we intend to transcend fate and impose our free will. However, in order for life tasks, personal strivings, and personal projects to be successful, it is very important that we be aware of our Moirae and carefully plan within our limits. For example, Palys and Little (1983) found that personal projects which were moderately difficult, enjoyable, and directed toward short-term goals resulted in individuals who reported greater levels of life satisfaction. To develop such goals requires self-awareness in relation to limitations and abilities.

Note also that motivational, purposive, and cognitive variables may be consistent with the Moirae, especially when they directly correspond to culturally and biologically defined developmental periods. Individuals in early adulthood who seek identity, vocation, and romantic relationships are engaged in life tasks that Erikson (1980) viewed as endemic to those in their teens and twenties. We therefore see that these cognitive constructs, although allowing for free choice, can also be constrained by developmental, social, and cultural forces beyond human control.

Researchers influenced by the pioneering humanistic psychologists for example, like Abraham Maslow and Carl Rogers, have also developed motivational, individual difference variables. Original humanistic psychologists such as Maslow emphasized that humans strive to reach their full potential. Maslow (1968) viewed this striving as a drive toward self-actualization directed in accordance to a hierarchy of needs, beginning with physiological sustenance and safety as keystones. When these needs are met then love and esteem needs arise until we are finally drawn toward fulfilling our unique potential through self-actualizing.

Maslow distinguished between what he termed *being values*, which encourage growth and enrichment of experience, and are found among self-actualizers, and *deficiency motives*, instigated by the need to fulfill a lack in one's life, and correspond with motives at the bottom of the hierarchy. Here again we see the hand of the Moirae at work. Deficiency motives arise from fundamental physiological and psychological needs that are as yet unsatisfied. As a result, they hinder a person's ability to act freely because basic motives are replacing a gap in life. Self-actualizers are characterized by generally accurate perceptions of reality, acceptance, spontaneity, creativity, autonomy, and transcendent experience. Individuals need these essential characteristics in order to discern the influence of fate in their own lives, and to subsequently feel unfettered by the biological, social, and cultural restraints impinging upon them.

Although one purpose of the original humanistic psychologists has been to directly address human nature and free will, greater numbers of contemporary researchers focus on individual differences in life functioning and experience. Humanistic research has therefore in many respects developed in parallel with the cognitive and trait approaches. For example, shortly after the development of Maslow's theory, a variety of personality measures were developed to assess levels of self-actualization. More recently, Csikszentmihalyi (1990) has extended Maslow's transcendent concept of peak experiences to examine what he calls *flow* experiences characterized by intrinsically satisfying and consciousness absorbing activities. Therefore, we see that humanistic psychologists emphasize the capacity for change while also acknowledging human contingencies (e.g., Maslow's hierarchy of needs); these themes also echo a teleological and fatalistic psychology.

Narrative Approaches

Some of the most interesting theoretical developments in personality theory today are taking place among researchers who apply the narrative approach. Narrative psychologists argue for a new root metaphor in the field of psychology (Sarbin, 1986). To explain the narrative approach it is first necessary to distinguish between two ways of understanding the world. Most psychologists conduct research according to what Bruner (1986) labels a *paradigmatic mode* of thought, that is, through empiricism, logic and prediction, the criteria for scientific enterprise. However, we also comprehend the world through a *narrative mode* where, through the elements of story structure, we attempt to understand human desire, motivation, and intention over time. In this view, logic and correspondence with veridical reality are superseded by the artistic endeavor in revealing larger truths about human existence. Narrative psychologists treat human lives as stories with settings, characters, scripts, and plots that are organized over time. McAdams (1999) has identified "integrative themes" from which narrative psychologists regard *the self* as defined through evolving stories each person tells by cohering disparate experiences into a culturally embedded narrative. Through the storytelling we proceed to build intimacy and community; but psychologists also warn that the stories can either be psychologically healthy or destructive.

Narrative psychology has its roots in the psychoanalytic approach in a number of ways. For example, McAdams (1999) asserts that Adler, Murray, Erikson, and Jung all implicitly made narrative assumptions when tackling the psychology of human existence. The narrative approach is compelling because it integrates the two key themes of personality psychology. As discussed earlier, Buss (1999) claims that personality theories attempt primarily to explain either human nature or individual differences. We can conceive the narrative psychological method as the combination of the individual difference approach with transcendent themes as those in Jung's theory of the collective unconscious.

Let us examine one of the leading narrative theories in the contemporary literature and see how it can be viewed in the light of a teleological, fatalistic theory like the Moirae. McAdams (1993) has contributed a narrative theory of human identity and development in his textbook *The Person* (2001). McAdams' theory begins with Erikson's concept of identity formation being inherently linked to adolescent development when the teenager begins thinking, "Who am I?" McAdams asserts that this period is the beginning of a person's construction of a life story which is also contingent on his/her cognitive development. Piaget (1936) has shown that, only by adolescence are we able to think in formal operational terms, that is, when we possess the ability to cognitively construct our worlds in abstract and idealistic ways instead of only in concrete operational terms characteristic of childhood years. Such cognitive development is combined with cultural and social pressures that move us toward the development of identity during adolescence. "What do you want to be?" and "What do you believe?" become questions that the adolescent faces because of biological, cognitive, and social factors. McAdams argues that identity is a "psychosocial construction" whereby the person seeks coherence in life through story structures that have meaning within a cultural context. Therefore, variables such as gender, race, ethnicity, historical period, and culture impinge on the definition of self through the construction of the life story.

We can immediately observe a connection to the Moirae in McAdams' theory through his application of Erikson's developmental stages and thus the teleological, epigenetic principle. We also know that Piaget linked childhood cognitive development to biological development (also rooted in the Moirae). Furthermore, our identity and life story are dependent on culture, gender, and race, variables under which, at birth, we are unable to exert free will.

McAdams has discovered that the narratives we construct conform to particular themes and character structures. The themes uncovered by McAdams reveal patterns of story construction which Jung and Campbell attribute to the human collective unconscious. As McAdams himself notes, story typologies date at least back to Aristotle's time when he described four basic typologies: comedy, tragedy, romance, and irony. This effort to classify stories has been an interdisciplinary effort throughout time with philosophers, theologians, literary scholars, and psychologists taking part.

McAdams and others have identified thematic lines, such as *agency* and *communion* within the story structures of people's life narratives. Agentic themes emphasize self-mastery, power, achievement, and status and communal themes exemplify love, caring, togetherness, and communication (McAdams, Hoffman, Mansfield, & Day, 1996). McAdams also asserts that these narrative themes can be used to define an *imago*, an idealized image of the self, or if you will, the main character in the life narrative (McAdams, 1993). Levels of agency and communion can be found in various imago types and can be classified into categories (McAdams, 1993). Notice that when conceptualized in this manner, narrative themes could be treated in a similar way as trait variables. However, McAdams (2001) is careful to note that these classifications should be viewed within an unfolding story structure and not simply as static classifications.

More important from our perspective as mentioned above, are the efforts of Campbell, who adopted the Jungian notions of the collective unconscious and archetypes in order to discern consistent and significant themes in stories and myths. An important archetype introduced in chapter two is Campbell's (1949) identification of "the hero" across cultures. The hero's separation, initiation, and return in legends, myths, and religious stories of various cultures is thematic in the individual's psychological pattern. Using the terminology of McAdams, it constitutes a type imago. Campbell has furthermore shown that these narrative structures are inherent to our personality. Let us also remember that Jung viewed the archetypes as comprising the collective unconscious, which he presumed to be a *biological* structure. We find further evidence of an intrinsic link to narrative in that stories as vehicles of expression and meaning have been told across history, and that storytelling is embedded in everyday culture (Howard, 1989; Linde, 1993; McAdams, 1999).

We should note other similarities of the Moirae with the narrative approach. As stated in chapter two, the Moirae are best conceptualized as a process, not an entity, and they operate simultaneously on many levels of consciousness; the construction of a life narrative is also an ongoing process. We see this in McAdams' emphasis on not treating the imago as a personality type but rather as conceptualizing it as a developing character in an unfolding narrative. Although McAdams focuses on the conscious expression of stories, it is likely that most of our narrative constructions take place beyond current awareness and we retain only conscious knowledge of the product itself. Finally, the Moirae can be perceived as a new "root metaphor" for psychology in the same way that the narrative psychologist seeks accurate conceptualizations of the person. However, the Moirae offers a meta-theory which unites the paradigmatic and narrative modes, provides an explanation of human nature, and leaves room for individual difference research.

Despite the important new developments in this line of research and similarities with the Moirae, narrative psychologists have yet to provide an integrative and comprehensive explanation as to *why* we construct our stories (apart from the psychological need to create meaning in our lives). From the perspective of the Moirae, I strongly suspect that we are drawn to the stories we create; they already exist within our biology and the cultural context. A teleological view of the narrative perspective indicates that stories are a physical part of the universe manifested genetically and hence through the biological structure of the human brain. Our consciousness gives rise to the physical structure of our fate, and ultimately, we can view the results of the Moirae in our daily psychology and behavior. In the prevailing psychological world view, narrative research is not accepted as evidence of preexisting storytelling structures at birth. Instead, psychologists have decided that stories are generated after events take place but there is no definitive reason to presume that that assumption is true.

Clinical Interventions and the Potential for Change

We have already discussed the small beacon of hope that illuminates the potential for human change and the exercise of free will. However, this chapter has provided us with further issues to consider. The trait perspective apparently provides little insight into possibilities for change. As Quackenbush (2001) has shown, a pre-empirical assumption of the five-factor model is stability across the lifespan. Such a model of human behavior allows scant discussion of the potential for life changes, but it does help to explain consistency across the life-span. However, the individual difference cognitive variables operate somewhat differently. Because variables such as life tasks, personal projects, and personal strivings are malleable and thus can alter, depending on developmental or environmental factors, the factors themselves can inspire greater opportunities for change (Little, 1999). We see that the Moirae can provide us with an answer to the *why* question. Fate can create our opportunities for freedom and change through the intersection of biological, developmental, and situational determinants. Possibilities for true change and personal growth arrive at these critical junctures in our lives; it is therefore important to be vigilant to their arrival in order to seize them if we see fit.

There are obvious opportunities as well as noted limitations for those working in the counseling environment. If a client is embroiled in a web of deterministic variables, a discussion of personal goals is probably futile. However, the client whose chains of fate have been loosened through medication, a life change, or other similar circumstance, now has a wonderful opportunity to embark on a different life course. For example, we find that depression is best treated with a combination of anti-depressant medication and counseling therapy. Once a person is freed from the biological tomb of depression, therapeutic advice can then provide a window of opportunity.

Humanistic therapies are also based on prospects for personal growth and free will, even if research in this area at times treats variables in a static, trait-like manner. The work of theorists and practitioners like Rogers and Maslow have generated decades of valuable literature on the possibilities for human change. Humanistic psychologists have provided valuable insights into the possibilities for change, but their almost exclusive focus on the issue of growth has impeded some humanistic-oriented theorists and practitioners from investigating the contingencies of human existence. This view of human nature is perhaps best summarized by Maslow (1968) who aptly stated, "A teacher or culture doesn't create a human being. It doesn't implant within him the ability to love, or to be curious, or to philosophize, or to symbolize, or to be creative. Rather it permits, or fosters, or encourages, or helps what exists in embryo to become real and actual" (p. 161). But the humanistic perspective leaves us wanting. What is it then that infuses us with the ability to love, to be curious, to philosophize, to symbolize, and to create? Beneficially, the Moirae not only expose the contingencies of human existence but also the possibilities for change.

Of the theories existing to date, narrative theories present exciting possibilities to simultaneously discuss growth and change while acknowledging the concrete limitations of life from a therapeutic and research perspective. As McAdams (2001) has noted, many psychoanalytic theorists see the construction of a healthy life story as central to making sense of one's life. Stories help those experiencing trauma find meaning in their lives (Pennebaker, 1997; Pennebaker & Beall, 1986; White & Epson, 1990). Because of developments in narrative theory and within psychoanalytic therapy, an entire subfield of narrative-oriented therapies has arisen (White & Epston, 1990). Such developments are not surprising. We have already noted that storytelling is endemic to the human condition, and that the stories we tell ourselves impact on our emotional and psychological well-being. The process of reinterpreting life events within a different narrative can alter our perspective of the world. This idea has borne fruit within the therapeutic arena as well as in the research domain. For example, McAdams, Diamond, de St. Aubin, and Mansfield (1997) identify *commitment stories* often present in the lives of highly generative adults. Commitment stories are those in which the person constructing the story recognizes an early characteristic within themselves, which allows them to transcend misfortune. A commitment to a set of values enables them not only to rise above misfortune, but also to potentially dedicate themselves to improving conditions for future generations.

However, the same issues arise here as we saw with the establishment of life goals in a therapeutic context. Is the person able to reinterpret the events of their lives? Can a person find meaning in the supposedly chaotic events of their lives? Once again the person must be biologically, developmentally, and socially prepared to make such a shift in consciousness. These variables are often subject to fate. We even find acknowledgement of this among the clinical profession in what are termed the personality disorders (e.g. narcissistic personality disorder, histrionic personality disorder); these are notoriously difficult to treat compared to disorders where a biological component has clearly been identified and where therapy has greater success in conjunction with medication (e.g., depression, anxiety).

Finally, narrative therapies and research also teach us about the larger impact regarding the opportunities for exercising free will to alter and enrich our culture. Important fate variables such as historical period and culture provide us with the chance to interpret our own lives. These opportunities can be enriched through the available cultural myths and biographies that inspire and frame each person's life experience. If a culture provides rich and powerful narratives, then we should be able to observe and grasp many opportunities for meaning and growth. If instead we live in a fragmented culture where larger narratives and meaningful life stories are rare, or unknown because of a truncated educational process, then we are apt to find individuals who experience profound alienation or nihilistic feelings. The lack of accepted cultural narratives in our own society also highlights the need for narratives within minority communities and for women. The memoirs of members in these communities often illustrate a feeling of alienation from the larger culture.

Conclusion

In chapters six and seven we examined contemporary psychological research in the light of the fatalistic and teleological perspective of the Moirae. We noted that psychologists in personality psychology have sought an overarching theoretical construct in order to unify the field. The scope, range, and breadth of human behaviors that we try to explain in personality psychology are broad enough to encompass most research in psychology. By reinterpreting the theories and research in personality psychology in the light of the Moirae, we provide a framework that posits philosophical positions which unite all of psychology and identify teleological and fatalistic themes that transcend and unite all levels of analysis. As a result, we have found that a study of the Moirae not only provides a philosophical basis to interpret research in a broad way but that it also addresses human nature and examines the role of individual difference. Our final task is to concentrate the diverse themes presented here into one final question, which is, what does it mean to be human?

also to the physical universe. The attempt here has been to galvanize some of habits and processes in contemporary psychology and steer them toward a teleological and fatalistic explanation of the human condition.

The unconscious collective processes are expressed psychologically in a *personal future unconscious*. Thoughts and behaviors are molded by their teleological nature, and for each person destiny is manifested at the unconscious level. We are imparted with the Moirae from the natural universe *through* our biological, genetic structures inherited as physical and psychological attributes. Our genes collectively form a "soft predestination" whereby we contain *forces* that draw us into the future.

We have discussed how our Moirae phenomenologically possess us and can sometimes cause us to behave in irrational ways; further, these behaviors are often cyclical in nature. One exemplification of these features is the case of drug/alcohol addiction. However, we also noted that the foundation of biological, social, and cultural life, represented by cyclical processes, can be observed in many behaviors.

Finally, we have fully explored the issue of free will and its relation to fate. The Moirae do not dictate the prosaic details of everyday behaviors. Instead, they establish the parameters and the framework within which we exercise free will. Despite that human beings have grappled with the existence of free will and determinism, psychologists have seldom addressed the issue. The meta-theoretical framework of the Moirae presented here is indeed intended to advance and build on the discussion of the psychological relationship between free will and determinism.

The meta-theoretical approach of the Moirae allows us to address how fate and destiny influence drug addiction, spirituality, sexual activity, and aggression. Important too, is that this meta-theoretical approach encompasses applied issues as well as psychological theories and research through the filter of philosophical reasoning.

Implications

What are the implications of adopting the Moirae as a meta-theoretical perspective for psychology? How does such a theory unify psychological research? How does it depart from traditional ideas in psychology? And, importantly, how should psychology students interpret human behavior?

We have characterized the human condition as teleological and fatalistic in nature; these processes usually operate outside of our awareness. We are each born to become someone. We possess a destiny. This idea radically departs from the standard view in psychology, yet it also serves to unite a disparate and fragmented field of study. An examination of contemporary psychology does not yield a particularly coherent set of interpreters of the human condition. The neuroscientist, social psychologist, and therapist seem to have precious little in common. Students cannot always make connections between these fields, and teachers at times struggle to elucidate how subfields can fit differently in the same framework. However, each subfield will often be regarded as the purview of psychology by most psychologists. When asked what unifies the field, many psychologists provide two answers. First, psychologists adopt a scientific approach in order to understand behavior and cognition, which requires data gathering and assumptions of causality. Second, our methodology for discerning the laws and principles in regard to human behavior and cognition are based on scientific methodology with an emphasis on laboratory experimentation. Despite the validity of the two assertions, they may not by themselves be adequate philosophical string to tie together the package of psychology.

The Moirae theory provides us with the bridge to unify psychological theory, research, and practice; furthermore, it connects us to the biological and physical world while simultaneously allowing for exploration into our spiritual, religious, and philosophical natures. The neuroscientist, social psychologist, and therapist are all welcome at the table. The student of psychology moreover has an enhanced ability to make connections among the various aspects in their own lives. What prevents us therefore from adopting this meta-theory? I would argue that the empirically-oriented, scientific training that most academic psychologists receive restricts us from seeking and finding connections between the various levels of psychology. We have been trained to employ a circumscribed set of methods in order to examine a narrow scope of problems. Such specificity in approach produces abundant research within each subfield of psychology, but is nevertheless problematical in that each subfield can become mired in its own assumptions. The outcome could be a fragmented view of psychology and an incoherent view of human existence.

A unified meta-theory such as the Moirae would provide us with a new understanding of human nature; it would unify the diverse research areas and theories and allow us to address important applied topics. In other words, the teleological and fatalistic explanation that elucidated this work also unifies and provides direction for psychological theory, research, and therapy.

Individuals who struggle against addiction or violence in their lives can begin to understand the cyclical patterns that have controlled them and by so doing perhaps shift in a different direction. Those who cope with mental or physical disorders can better understand the strength of deterministic forces underlying their condition. Those who are fortunate enough to not be troubled by these issues can more easily recognize the fundamental direction their lives may take. We can more deeply understand that indeed we have a destiny, and it is incumbent upon us to take active measures to fulfill or modify that destiny, whether it relates to career, relationships, or other pursuits. Finally, by understanding the contingencies of our existence, we may be better equipped to pursue the forgiveness of others and the redemption that we all seek.

Future Directions

Human beings have sought unifying principles since the dawn of our existence, and so too we ask what binds us together in the human experience. The result of a fundamental drive to know has produced philosophy, science, and religion. In this work I have attempted to produce a meta-theory that can unite psychology. However, other principles with larger implications, as to how we regard the human condition, have also been delineated in this process.

Is the self to be perceived as individualistic and isolated, or as an entity embedded in a larger community? Edith Hamilton (1963), in *The Greek Way,* outlines key elements distinguishing the Greek "way" from our contemporary *lebenswelt.* She thinks that the central distinction between Greek and contemporary thinking is that, while contemporary culture emphasizes the individual as a unique character, the Greeks viewed individuals as essentially the same, and more importantly, as part of a larger whole. One is struck by the similarity between psychological scientists' effort to identify similarities in human nature, by basing the science on aggregate data and statistical analysis, and the Greek philosophical concern with the common condition of all humans. This Greek characteristic of emphasizing human life and its relation to the larger universe is observed in Greek architecture, drama, and philosophy. Ironically, psychology first developed as a science out of the Westernized, individualistic view, which is part and parcel of the history of the United States in particular. However, psychology has increasingly moved toward understanding the relationship between the individual and his or her context, especially socially and culturally.

Such a shift in perspective has many important practical applications. For example, a movement within clinical psychology (i.e., community psychology) emphasizes how the role of the local community intervenes in treating mental disorders. Considered in conjunction with our previous related discussions regarding the success of self-change, we can see that it is not an individual issue but rather is rooted in biology, the person's social network, and the culture. The Moirae's emphasis on our connection to biology and the collective archetype of unconsciousness shows that we are connected, and that change is not merely a question of personal will.

The Moirae also have larger implications for the relationship between psychology and spirituality, religion, philosophy, literature, art, and other diverse fields of study. Many of the principles discussed here have an immediate impact, especially on sociology, anthropology, criminology, and political science. As we begin to examine fundamental principles underlying diverse areas of inquiry, we may stumble onto particular themes or concepts (and archetypal structures) that unify and represent the human experience. In chapter three we discussed the circle as metaphor for the human experience, including the biological cycles that impel us and focus our lives. The circle is central to diverse fields as mathematics, astronomy, biology, chemistry, music, literature, art, and religion, and may possibly be the unifying principle we have been looking for since our time began. Perhaps the present inquiry will also inspire others to seek concepts that unite and symbolize the human experience.

I conclude this discussion of the Moirae with the hope that we as researchers, analysts, and students proceed with an infinite curiosity to explore the minutiae of our existence, and concurrently to also develop a broader knowledge of human behavior. May we not only seek unifying principles in psychology, but also reach toward a new dawn for understanding what it does truly mean to be human.

References

Adorno, T. W., Frenkel-Brunswick, E., Levinson, D. J., & Sanford, R. N. (1950). *The authoritarian personality*. New York: Harper & Row.

Allport, G. (1937). *Personality: A psychological interpretation*. New York: Holt, Rinehart, & Winston.

Allport, G. W. (1961). *Pattern and growth in personality*. New York: Holt, Rinehart, & Winston.

Allsop, S. & Saunders, B. (1989). Relapse and alcohol problems. In M. Gossop (Ed.), *Relapse and addictive behaviour* (pp. 11–40). London: Routledge.

Altemeyer, B. (1981). *Right-wing authoritarianism*. Manitoba, Canada: University of Manitoba Press.

———. (1988). *Enemies of freedom*. San Francisco, CA: Jossey-Bass.

Asch, S. (1956). Studies of independence and conformity: A minority of one against a unanimous majority. *Psychological Monographs, 70(9),* (whole no. 416).

Averill, J. R., & Nunley, E. P. (1993). Grief as an emotion and as a disease: A social-constructionist perspective. In M. S. Stroebe, W. Stroebe, & R. O. Hansson (Eds.), *Handbook of Bereavement* (pp. 77–90). London & New York: Cambridge University Press.

Baumeister, R.F. (1997). *Evil: Inside human violence and cruelty*. New York: W.H. Freeman.

Bowlby, J. (1969). *Attachment and loss: Vol. I. attachment*. New York: Basic Books.

Brown, R. (1989). Relapses from a gambling perspective. In M. Gossop (Ed.), *Relapse and addictive behaviour* (pp. 107–132). London: Routledge.

Bruner, J. S. (1986) *Actual minds, possible worlds*. Cambridge, MA: Harvard University Press.

Buss, D. M. (1997). Human nature and individual differences: The evolution of human personality. In L. Pervin & O.P. John (Eds.), *Handbook of Personality* (2nd ed., pp. 31–56). New York: Guilford Press.

Buss, D. (1999). Adaptive individual differences revisited. *Journal of Personality, 67(2),* 259–264.

Campbell, J. (1949). *The hero with a thousand faces*, New York: Bollingen.

———. (1988). *The power of myth*. New York: Doubleday.

Cantor, N., & Zirkle, S. (1990). Personality, cognition, and purposive behavior. In L. Pervin (Ed.), *Handbook of personality: Theory and research* (pp. 135–164). New York: Guilford Press.

Carlson, N. R. (1991). *Physiology of behavior* (4th ed.). Newton, MA: Allyn and Bacon.

Cattell, R. B. (1945). The description of personality: Principles and findings in a factor analysis. *American Journal of Psychology, 58*, 69–90.

Chomsky, N. (1966). *Cartesian linguistics.* New York: Harper Row.

Cialdini, R. B., (2001). *Influence* (4th ed.). New York: HarperCollins College Publishers.

Cooper, J., & Scalise, C. J. (1974). Dissonance produced by deviations from life-styles: The interaction of Jungian typology and conformity. *Journal of Personality and Social Psychology, 29*, 566–571.

Costa, P. T., Jr., & McCrae, R. R. (1992). Normal personality assessment in clinical practice: The NEO personality inventory. *Psychological Assessment, 4*, 5–13.

Cotterell, A. (1989). *The Macmillan illustrated encyclopedia of myths & legends.* New York: Macmillan.

Csikszentmihalyi, M. (1990). *Flow: The psychology of optimal experience.* New York: Harper and Row.

Dawkins, R. (1976). *The selfish gene.* New York: Oxford University Press.

———. (2006). *The God delusion.* London: Bantam Press.

de Waal, F. (1996). *Good natured: The origins of right and wrong in humans and other animals.* Cambridge, MA: Harvard University Press.

Doty R. M., Peterson, B. E., & Winter, D. G. (1991). Threat and authoritarianism in the United States, 1978–1987. *Journal of Personality and Social Psychology, 61*, 629–640.

Eisenberger, R. & Shank, D. (1985). Personal work ethic and effort training affect cheating. *Journal of Personality and Social Psychology, 49*, 520–528.

Emerson, R. W. (1981). The poet. In C. Bode & M. Cowley's (Eds.) *The portable Emerson* (241–265). New York: Penguin Books. (Original work published 1844).

———. (1981). Fate. In C. Bode & M. Cowley's (Eds.) *The portable Emerson* (pp. 346–374). New York: Penguin Books. (Original work published 1860).

Emmons, R. (1992). Abstract versus concrete goals: Personal striving level, physical illness, and psychological well-being. *Journal of Personality and Social Psychology, 62*, 292–300.

Erikson, E. H. (1980). *Identity and the life cycle.* New York: W.W. Norton.

Eysenck, H. (1967). *The biological basis of personality.* Springfield, IL: Charles C. Thomas.

Feldman, S. & Stenner, K. (1997). Perceived threat and authoritarianism. *Political Psychology, 18*, 741–770.

Fitzgerald, F. S. (1991). *The great Gatsby* (M. Bruccoli, Trans.), Cambridge: Cambridge University Press. (Original work published 1925).

Freud, S. (2006). *The interpretation of dreams.* (A. Underwood, Trans.). Toronto, Ontario: Penguin Books Limited. (Original work published 1899).

———. (1961). The ego and the id. In J. Strachey (Ed. and Trans.), *The standard edition of the complete psychological works of Sigmund Freud* (Vol. 19, pp. 12–66). London: Hogarth Press. (Original work published 1923).

———. (1984). *Leonardo da Vinci: A memory of his childhood.* (A. Tyson, Ed.) London: Routledge. (Original work published 1910).

———. (1995). Beyond the pleasure principle. In P. Gay (Ed.), *The Freud Reader* (pp 594–626), London: Vintage (Original work published 1920).

———. (1995). *The dissolution of the Oedipus complex.* In P. Gay (Ed.), *The Freud Reader* (pp 661–666). London: Vintage (Original work published 1924).

Geen, R. G., & Donnerstein, E. (Eds.), *Human aggression: Theories, research, and implications for social policy*. San Diego: Academic Press.

Gergen, K. J. (1991). *The saturated self: Dilemmas of identity in contemporary life*. New York: Basic Books.

Gershon, E. S., Berrettini, W. H., Nurnberger, J. I., Jr., & Goldin, L. R. (1989). Genetic studies of affective illness. In J. J. Mann (Ed.), *Models of depressive disorders: Psychological, biological, and genetic perspectives* (pp. 109–142). New York: Plenum.

Goldberg, E. (1981). Role of the right hemisphere in the formation of linguistic skills. *Journal of Educational Neuropsychology, 1,* 1–15.

———. (1990). *Contemporary neuropsychology and the legacy of Luria*. Hillsdale, NJ: Lawrence Erlbaum.

Goodwin, F. K., Wirz-Justice, A., & Wehr, T. A. (1982). Evidence that the pathophysiology of depression and the mechanism action of antidepressant drugs both involve alterations in circadian rhythms. In E. Costa, & G. Racagni (Eds). *Advances in Biochemical Psychopharmacology, Vol. 32, Typical and Atypical Antidepressants: Clinical Practice* (pp. 1–11). New York: Raven Press.

Gray, J. (1987). *The psychology of fear and stress* (2nd ed.).Cambridge: Cambridge University Press

Hall C. S. & Lindzey G. (1957). *Theories of personality*. New York: Wiley.

Hamilton, E. (1942). *Mythology*. Boston: Little, Brown and Company.

———. (1963). *The Greek way*. New York: W.W. Norton & Company.

Hastings, B. M. (2007). ROY G. BIV and the OCEAN: A heuristic metaphor for understanding the role of the five-factor model in personality research. *Theory & Psychology, 17,* 87–99.

Hastings, B. M. & Shaffer, B. A. (2005). Authoritarianism and sociopolitical attitudes in response to threats of terror, *Psychological Reports, 97,* 623–630.

Hastings, B. M. & Shaffer, B. A. (in press). Authoritarianism: The role of threat, evolutionary psychology, and the will to power, *Theory and Psychology*.

Hatab, L. J. (1990). *Myth and philosophy: A contest of truths*. La Salle, IL: Open Court.

Heatherton, T. F., Mahamedi, F., Striepe, M., Field, A., & Keel, P. (1997). A ten year longitudinal study of body weight, dieting, and eating disorder symptoms. *Journal of Abnormal Psychology, 106,* 117–125.

Heidegger, M. (1996). *Being and time*. (J. Stambaugh, Trans.). Albany, NY: State University of New York Press. (Original work published in 1953).

Henriques, G. (2003). The tree of knowledge system and the theoretical unification of psychology. *Review of General Psychology, 7(2),* 150–182.

Howard, G. S. (1989). *A tale of two stories: Excursions into a narrative approach to psychology*. Notre Dame, IN: Academic Press.

James, W. (1984). *Psychology: Briefer course*. (F. Burkhart, Ed.) Boston, MA: Harvard University Press. (Original work published in 1892).

———. (1996). *The thought and character of William James, Vol. 1.* (R. B. Perry, Ed.). Boston, MA: Harvard University Press. (Original work published in 1935).

Jung, C. (1973). *Synchronicity: An acausal connecting principle*. (R. F. C. Hull Trans.) Princeton, NJ: Princeton University Press. (Original work published in 1955).

———. (1971). Instinct and the unconscious. In J. Campbell (Ed.), *The Portable Jung* (pp. 47–58). New York: Penguin Books. (Original work published in 1919).

———. (1971). The structure of the psych. In J. Campbell (Ed.), *The Portable Jung* (pp. 23–46). New York: Penguin Books. (Original work published in 1927).

———. (1971). Aion: Phenomenology of the self. In J. Campbell (Ed.), *The Portable Jung* (pp. 139–162). New York: Penguin Books. (Original work published in 1951).

Jung, C. G. (1989). Memories, dreams, reflections. A. Jaffe (Ed.). Richard and Clara Winston (Trans.). New York: Vintage Books.

Kastenbaum, R., and Briscoe, L. (1975). The street corner: A laboratory for the study of life threatening behavior. *Omega, Journal of Death and Dying, 6*, 33–44.

Kazantzakis, N. (1960). *The last temptation of Christ.* New York: Simon & Schuster.

Kierkegaard, S. (1959). The journals of Kierkegaard. (Alexander Dru, Ed.). New York: Harper & Row. (Original 1843).

Ksir, C. J., Hart, C. L., & Ray, O. S. (2006). *Drugs, society, and human behavior.* Boston: McGraw-Hill.

Le Doux, J. (1992). Emotion as memory: Anatomical systems underlying indelible neural traces. In S.-A. Christianson (Ed.), *Handbook of emotion and memory: Research and theory.* (pp. 269–288). Hillsdale, NJ: Erlbaum.

Linde, C. (1993). *Life stories: The creation of coherence.* New York: Oxford University Press.

Little, B. R. (1989). Personal projects analysis: Trivial pursuits, magnificent obsessions, and the search for coherence. In D. Buss & N. Cantor (Eds.), *Personality psychology: Recent trends and emerging directions* (pp. 15–31). New York: Springer-Verlag.

————. (1999). Personality and motivation: Personal action and the cognitive evolution. In L. A. Pervin & O. P. John (Eds.), *Handbook of personality theory and research* (2nd ed., pp. 501–524). New York: Guilford Press.

Lorenz, K. (1963). *On aggression.* San Diego: Harcourt, Brace, and World.

Maccoby, E. E. (1988). Gender as a social category. *Developmental Psychology, 26*, 755–765.

Maisto, S. A., Galizio, M., & Connors, G. J. (1991). *Drug use and misuse.* New York: Harcourt Brace Jovanovich College Publishers.

Maslow, A. (1968). *Toward a psychology of being (*2nd ed.). New York: Van Nostrand.

Matthews, G., & Dreary, I. (1998). *Personality traits.* Cambridge, England: Cambridge University Press.

May, R. (1981). *Freedom and Destiny.* New York: W.W. Norton & Company.

Mayer, J. D. (2005). A tale of two visions: Can a new view of personality help integrate psychology? *American Psychologist, 60*, 294–307.

McAdams, D. P. (1993). *The stories we live by: Personal myths and the making of the self.* New York: William Morrow.

————. (1994). *The person: An integrated introduction to personality psychology* (2nd ed.). Fort Worth, TX: Harcourt.

————. (1999). Personal narratives and the life story. In Pervin, L., & John, O. (Eds.), *Handbook of Personality: Theory and Research* (2nd ed., pp. 478–500). New York: Guilford Press.

————. (2001). *The person: An integrated introduction to personality psychology* (3rd ed.). Fort Worth, TX: Harcourt.

McAdams, D. P., Diamond, A., de St. Aubin, E., & Mansfield, E. (1997). Stories of commitment: The psychosocial construction of generative lives. *Journal of Personality and Social Psychology, 72*, 678–694.

McAdams, D. P., Hoffman, B. J., Mansfield, E. D., & Day, R. (1996). Themes of agency and communion in significant autobiographical scenes. *Journal of Personality, 64*, 339–378.

McAdams, D. P. & Pals, J. L. (2006). A new big five: Fundamental principles for an integrative science of personality. *American Psychologist, 61(3)*, 204–217.

McCann, S. J. H. & Stewin, L. L. (1987). Threat, authoritarianism, and the power of U.S. presidents. *The Journal of Psychology, 121*, 149–157.

McCrae, R. R. & Costa, P. T., Jr. (1990). *Personality in adulthood.* New York: Guilford Press.

Milgram, S. (1974). *Obedience to authority.* New York: Harper & Row.

Mischel, W. (1974). Processes in delay of gratification. In L Berkowitz (Ed.), *Advances in experimental social psychology, Vol. 7* (pp. 249–292). San Diego, CA: Academic Press.

———. (1983). Delay of gratification as process and as a person variable in development. In D. Magnusson and V. P. Allen (Eds.), *Interactions in human development* (pp. 149–165). New York: Academic Press.

Murray, H. (1955). American Icarus, In A. Burton and R. E. Harris (Eds.), *Clinical Studies in Personality* (2nd ed., pp. 615–641). New York: Harper & Brothers.

Nettle, D. (2006). The evolution of personality variation in humans and other animals. *American Psychologist, 61,* 622–31.

Newberg, A., Alavi, A., Baime, M., Pourdehnad, M., Santanna, J., and d'Aquili, E. (2001). The measurement of regional cerebral blood flow during the complex cognitive task of meditation: A preliminary SPECT study. *Psychiatry Research: Neuroimaging, 106,* 113–122.

Newberg, A., D'Aquili, E., & Rause, V. (2001), *Why God won't go away: Brain science and the biology of belief.* New York: Ballantine Books.

Nietzsche, F. (1966). *Beyond Good and Evil.* (W. Kaufmann, Trans.), New York: Vintage. (Original work published 1886).

———. (1968). *Will to power.* (W. Kaufmann & R.J. Hollingdale, Trans.), New York: Vintage Books. (Original work published 1901).

———. (1982). *The portable Nietzsche.* (W. Kaufmann, Trans.), New York: Penguin. (Original work published 1882).

———. (2006). *Thus spake Zarathustra.* (T. Common, Trans.), El Paso, TX: Norte Press. (Original work published 1883–1885).

Norcross, J. C., Ratzin, A.C., & Payne, D. (1989). Ringing in the new year: The change processes and reported outcomes of resolutions. *Addictive Behaviors, 14*(2), 205–212.

Norman, R. M. G., & Watson, L. D. (1976). Extraversion and reactions to cognitive inconsistency. *Journal of Research in Personality, 10,* 446–456.

Norman, W. T., (1963). Toward an adequate taxonomy of personality attributes: Replicated factor structure in peer nominated personality ratings. *Journal of Abnormal and Social Psychology, 66,* 574–583.

Palys, T. S. & Little, B. R. (1983). Perceived life satisfaction and the organization of personal project systems. *Journal of Personality & Social Psychology, 44*(6), 1221–1230.

Pennebaker, J. W. (1997). Writing about emotional experiences as a therapeutic process. *Psychological Science, 8,* 162–166.

Pennebaker, J. W. & Beall, S. (1986). Confronting a traumatic event: Toward an understanding of inhibition and disease. *Journal of Abnormal Psychology, 95,* 274–281.

Pepper, S. (1942). *World hypotheses: A study in evidence.* Berkley, CA: University of California Press.

Piaget, J. (1936). *Origins of intelligence in the child.* London: Routledge & Kegan Paul.

Pinel, J. P. (2006). *Biopsychology.* Boston, MA: Allyn & Bacon.

Pinker, S. (1997). *How the mind works.* New York: W.W. Norton & Company.

Plato. (2006). *The republic.* (R. E. Allen, Trans.) New Haven, Connecticut: Yale University Press. (Original work published 360 B.C.).

Polivy, J. & Herman, P. C. (1999). Distress and eating: Why do dieters overeat? *International Journal of Eating Disorders, 26*(2), 153–164.

Polivy, J. & Herman, P. (2002). Causes of eating disorders. *Annual Reviews Psychology,* *53,* 187–213.

Prochaska, J. O., Velicer, W. F., Guadagnoli, E., Rossi, J., & DiClemente, C. C. (1991). Patterns of change: A dynamic typology applied to smoking cessation. *Multivariate Behavioral Research, 26,* 83–107.

Quackenbush, S. W. (2001). Trait stability as a noncontingent truth: A pre-empirical critique of McCrae and Costa's stability thesis. *Theory & Psychology,* 11, 818–836.

Reginster, B. (2006). *The affirmation of life: Nietzsche on overcoming nihilism.* Cambridge, MA: Harvard University Press.

Rosenzweig, M. & Leiman, A. (1989). *Physiological psychology.* New York: Random House.

Sarbin, T. R. (1986). The narrative as a root metaphor for psychology. In T. R. Sarbin (Ed.), *Narrative psychology: The storied nature of human conduct* (pp. 3–21). New York: Praeger.

Sartre, J. (1983). *Being and nothingness.* (H. Barnes, Trans.). New York: Washington Square Press. (Original work published 1943).

Sartre, J. P. (1965). *Essays in existentialism.* Secaucus, NJ: The Citadel Press.

———. (1981). *The family idiot: Gustave Flaubert, 1821–1857 (Vol. 1)* (C. Cosman, Trans). Chicago: University of Chicago Press.

———. (2004). Existentialism. In G. Marino's (Ed.), *Basic writings of existentialism* (pp.341–367). New York: The Modern Library. (Original work published 1957) .

Schneider, K. J. (1998). Toward a science of the heart: Romanticism and the revival of psychology. *American Psychologist,* 53(3), 277–289.

Scorsese, M. (Director), & Ufland, H. (Executive Producer). (1988). *The last temptation of Christ* [Motion Picture]. United States: Universal Pictures.

Scully, D. (1990). *Understanding sexual violence: A study of convicted rapists.* Boston, MA: Unwin-Hyman Press.

Shaffer, B. A. & Hastings, B. M. (2004). Self-esteem, authoritarianism, and democratic values in the face of threat. *Psychological Reports, 95,* 311–316.

Solomon, R. L. (1977). An opponent-process theory of acquired motivation: the affective dynamics of addiction. In J.D. Maser & M. Seligman, (Eds.) *Psychopathology: Experimental models* (pp. 66–103). San Francisco, CA: Freeman.

Sue, D., Sue, D. W., Sue, S. (2000). *Understanding abnormal behavior* (6th ed.). Boston, MA: Houghton Mifflin Company.

Tajfel, H. (1978). The psychological structure of intergroup relations. In H. Tajfel (Ed.), *Differentiation between social groups: Studies in the social psychology of intergroup relations.* London: Academic Press.

Thoreau H. D. (1993). *Civil disobedience and other essays.* New York: Dover Publications Inc. (Original work published 1862).

Thoreau, H. D. (1996). *The nature writings of Henry David Thoreau.* Ann Arbor: Tally Hall Press. (Original work published 1854).

Thorne, B. M. & Henley, T. B. (2005). *Connections in the history and systems of psychology.* Boston: Houghton Mifflin Company.

Tupes, E. C. & Cristal, R. E. (1961). Recurrent personality factors based on trait ratings. USAF ASD technical report no.61–97. (reprinted in *Journal of Personality,* 1992, *60,* 225–251).

Walker, L. E. (1984). *The battered woman syndrome.* New York: Springer Publications.

White, M. & Epston, D. (1990). *Narrative means to therapeutic ends.* New York: Doubleday.

Wilson, E. O. (1978). *On human nature.* Cambridge, MA: Cambridge University Press.

Wittgenstein, L. (1953) *Philosophical investigations* (G. E. M. Anscombe, Trans.). New York: Macmillan.

Wright, R. (1994). *The moral animal: The new science of evolutionary psychology.* New York: Vintage Books.

Zuckerman, M. (1991). *Psychobiology of personality.* Cambridge: Cambridge University Press.

———. (1995). Good and bad humors: Biochemical bases of personality and its disorders. *Psychological Science, 6,* 325–332.

Index

"fundamental choice," 43–44
"fundamental project," 56–57
future unconscious, 19–20, 60
future unconscious, personal, 16–19,
    24, 58, 61, 64, 98

gambling analogy, 61–62
Gandhi, M., 65
Gatsby, 39
The Gay Science, 47–48
gender, 24–27
genes, 53–54
genetic basis of Moirae, 19
Gergen, K. J., 65
Goethe, J. W., 6
Goldberg, E., 86
Goodwin, F. K., 34
grand theory of personality, 83
gratification, delay of, 38–39
Gray, J., 87
Greek heroes, 59
Greek mythology, 24, 73, 97–98
Greeks: and limitations of life, 61
Greek tragedy, 4–5
The Greek Way, 100
grief, 23
"Grim Reaper," 21–22
"ground plan," 75
group consensus, 82
group identification, 82

Hall, C. S., 69–70
Hamilton, E., 5, 100
Hatab, L. J., 4, 20, 24, 61
Heidegger, M., 22, 55
Helen of Troy, 5
Herman, P. C., 53, 54
hero archetype, 47, 72, 93
hero myth, 17
Hitler, Adolf, 6
homeostasis, 35
Homer, 5
human ancestry, 77
human development, eight stages of, 18
humanistic therapies, 94
humanistic variables, 89–91
human life, a new view of, 97
human social structure, 80
Icarus complex, 73
I Ching, 5

id, 55
identity formation, 92
idiographic research, 88–89
The Iliad, 5, 80
imago, 93
implications of meta-theory, 98–99
individual, emphasis on, 8–9, 100
individual differences, 85
individuation, 76
"integrative themes," 91
"Integrity versus Despair," 75
The Interpretation of Dreams, 33
irony, 92

James, William, 3, 26
Jesus, life of, 44–47, 48
Jocasta, 5
Joseph, story of, 5
Jung, C.: 15, 18, 69, 70, 92; and
    archetypes, 72; and collective
    unconscious, 93; and the self, 74,
    76; and synchronicity, 74; and
    unconscious, 71–72

Kant, Immanuel, 10
Kastenbaum, R., 22
Kazantzakis, Nikos, 46
Kierkegaard, S., 13
"know thyself," 9

Lachesis, 4
Laius, 4–5
"language acquisition device," 10
The Last Temptation of Christ, 46
lebenswelt, 3, 6, 8–9, 100
Leibniz, G. W., 10
Leonardo da Vinci: A Memory of His
    Childhood, 56
lexical hypothesis, 86
libido, 24, 75
life cycles, 31
life meaning and purpose, 82
life tasks, 90
life-world, 3
Lindzey, G., 69–70
Little, B. R., 90

maladaptive ritualistic behaviors, 35
Mansfield, E., 95
Mary, mother of Jesus, 45